THE
VICTORY

THE VICTORY

HE RESTORETH MY SOUL

CHERYL T. REMICK

XULON PRESS

Xulon Press
555 Winderley Pl, Suite 225
Maitland, FL 32751
407.339.4217
www.xulonpress.com

xulon
PRESS

Paperback ISBN-13: 979-8-86850-564-5
Ebook ISBN-13: 979-8-86850-565-2

I have been blessed to pastor Cheryl Remick at Right Direction Church in Louisiana and have seen her faithfulness as she gives of her time and talents to ministry both within the walls of our church as well as to the outside community. Cheryl's love of the Lord and of people is contagious. In The Victory, Cheryl shares Biblical principles that she has learned to live out through over 30 years serving the Lord. Cheryl explains these principles in an engaging and easy to understand way. I know you will be blessed as you read about Cheryl's journey with God and the experiences she has had with her husband Paul as they serve as missionaries to Africa. And, most importantly, you will be encouraged in your own walk with Jesus to live a life of complete and absolute freedom.

- PASTOR DEREK P. BUCHERT
Right Direction Church

It is with great joy and gratitude that I introduce this remarkable collection of experiences and teachings from Cheryl Remick, a dedicated missionary of the Kitega Community Centre Uganda.

Within these pages, you will find a collection of experiences that illuminate the essence of what it means to live out one's faith in action. Cheryl's journey is not just a personal narrative but a vibrant tapestry woven with the lives of countless individuals whose stories have intersected with hers. Each account reflects the heart of striving to build the Kingdom of God, where love transcends boundaries, hope flourishes, and lives are forever changed.

To all who take part in this journey—your efforts will truly be blessed. Cheryl has nurtured hope and made a lasting difference in the lives of many. May these stories inspire you to continue spreading kindness and light in the world.

With gratitude,
DAVID CLEMY
Kitega Community Centre, Uganda.

In this book " The Victory" by "Cheryl T Remick" you will find hope for healing and restoration through the power of the Holy Spirit and the Word of God. Cheryl shares out of a deep well of experiences of extreme hurt and betrayal. Having known her for nearly two decades, I will attest to her strong reliance upon God and His Word above her own "feelings and opinions" to walk in VICTORY over the lies and brutal attacks of the enemy. I encourage you to read this book and allow God to lead YOU to victory.

~ **Dr Denny Nissley**
Founder & Executive Director
Christ In Action

Psalm 23

"*The Lord is my shepherd; I shall not want. He maketh me lie down in green pastures: he leadeth me beside the still waters.*

He restoreth my soul; *he leadeth me in the path of righteousness for his name's sake.*

Yea, though I walk through the valley of the shadow of death, I will fear no evil: for thou art with me; thy rod and thy staff they comfort me.

Thou preparest a table before me in the presence of mine enemies: thou anointest my head with oil; my cup runneth over.

Surely goodness and mercy shall follow me all the days of my life: and I will dwell in the house of the LORD forever."

This book is dedicated to every wounded
soul that is longing to be healed.

May the Lord encourage you as His Word comes alive within you.
There truly is hope for emotional, physical,
and spiritual healing in your life.

TABLE OF CONTENTS

Introduction. xiii

Chapter One: My Journey. 1

Chapter Two: Shocking Truths 9

Chapter Three: Desperate Measures 15

Chapter Four: Changing My Focus 19

Chapter Five: Deep Wounds and Generational Curses. 23

Chapter Six: Forgiveness and Peace. 27

Chapter Seven: Laying the Foundation. 35

Chapter Eight: Revelation of the Bowls 39

Chapter Nine: Heart and Soul 49

Chapter Ten: Isolation. 55

Chapter Eleven: Renewing Your Mind 59

Chapter Twelve: Overcoming .65

Chapter Thirteen: Wisdom to Know the Difference 73

Chapter Fourteen: Power in the Blood 81

Chapter Fifteen: Dunamis, Miracle Working Power 89

Chapter Sixteen: Knowledge & Authority in Christ. 97

Chapter Seventeen: Application and Activation 107

Chapter Eighteen: Scriptures to Declare Over Your Life 113

Chapter Nineteen: Testimony of the Power of Prayer 117

Chapter Twenty: Just as Elijah - Desiring Death in Despair 121

INTRODUCTION

Through the years, I have had a passion to see people set free from the things that hold them back in life. I was once one of those people, so I can attest to the desperate need to be set free. Once I had the revelation and the freedom that came through Christ, nothing was going to stop me from sharing how it can be achieved.

I have taught this revelation to many people over the years, both in the United States and in Africa. My intention is that brand new believers, as well as seasoned Christians, will be able to see and understand through the scriptures just how much power they have in Christ. There truly is hope for emotional, physical, and spiritual healing in every area of our lives.

I started writing this book while sitting in the Kitega Village in Uganda, Africa. My husband Paul and I were in Africa for seven weeks ministering in Churches and to individuals throughout Kenya and Uganda about overcoming the works of the devil, breaking generational curses, and healing the deepest wounds in their souls- wounds that have affected them most, if not all, of their lives.

Seasoned Pastors, Bishops, Priests, and Lay Ministers had asked me to leave my teachings with them because they wanted to share this with everyone they possibly could. Unfortunately, I only had one printed copy of my notes that I carried with me throughout our travels in their countries.

My notes alone would not help them anyway because they were just a guideline for me. I promised each of the leaders that I would find a way to get my notes written down where they could use it in their ministries. That is when I realized that my notes needed to be in book form. Having no knowledge of what "book form" entailed, I started typing. The next thing I knew, a precious woman of God whom I had the honor of meeting in a bridal shop almost two years earlier made a post about getting unfinished projects done this year, and she even mentioned a book! This was a confirmation indeed. There I was at 58 years old in Africa starting my first book.

By sharing part of my own testimony, I will lay the foundation so we can reach the power source of complete healing, which is Holy Scriptures. Everyone's experiences and wounds are different, but God's Word covers them all. The things I share are in no way intended to bring negative attention to anyone I write about. Names have been changed to not expose people or their families unnecessarily.

I pray that as you are reading this book you will glean what is needed for yourself and share what you can to help others.

My life changed dramatically through the revelations that I received in God's Word, and I know that yours can too. I had no idea that I could be restored in the depths of my soul and be set free physically, spiritually, and emotionally. Being able to enjoy life to the fullest seemed like only a dream. May the Lord encourage you as His Word comes alive within the depths of your soul as it did in mine. I believe that complete victory is in your near future.

Most of the scripture references are from the King James Version of the Bible unless otherwise noted. I will add words in parentheses as needed for clarity.

ACKNOWLEDGMENTS

First and foremost, I want to acknowledge the Lord for the
great revelations that He has given to me for this book.

My husband Paul for being the greatest
cheerleader and my best friend.

Pastors Derek and Bonnie Buchert for their
ongoing encouragement and prayers.

Michelle Fortier for the countless hours
spent through this entire process.

Regina Goettz for holding my hand the whole way through.

Joanna Renz and Gayle Crovetto for the
final push across the finish line.

To a special person who invested in this project, I am forever grateful.

And for many dear friends that graciously read
the manuscript and provided feedback.

You have all been instrumental in this book.

CHAPTER ONE
MY JOURNEY

My journey with the Lord began in 1987 when I was introduced to Jesus Christ by a very brave soldier in the Lord's army. He had his work cut out for him because I was not going to be an easy convert.

Prior to my salvation, I was an angry, bitter person. When I was a young girl, my mother was in a terrible boating accident. The accident caused her much grief and pain. The injuries she suffered were so severe that amputation of her leg seemed the only possibility. Thankfully, an amazing orthopedic surgeon was able to save her leg but not without many surgeries, extreme pain, and extensive therapy. This very independent woman became confined to a chair and then a polio brace just to be able to support the bones in her leg. It was many years before she gained a little independence back. As of today, at eighty years old, my mother is by far the strongest woman I have ever met.

Whenever a tragedy happens to someone, everyone in the home is affected. The daily routines are changed, emotions run high, and strife finds a way in the door. I watched as my parents' marriage began to deteriorate, and it eventually ended in divorce. They were married just a few months shy of twenty years. My younger siblings struggled the most because being very young, they were still living at home. My older sister and I were both married, so we suffered the heartache and ongoing battle from outside.

Divorce not only hurts the adults involved, it also creates deep wounds in the children as they are put in the middle of the biggest battle they have ever faced.

A few months prior to my parents' separation, I found myself married and pregnant at sixteen years old. My husband was nineteen. Seeing all the strife that was in my home growing up, I became very controlling and even cruel with my words to my husband. He did not deserve to be treated that way. No one does. The vulgarity that came out of my mouth regularly is now most embarrassing to even admit.

In 1987, my husband and I got involved in a business venture where we met a man named Keith who has since gone home to be with the Lord. He was a Christian and had a very gentle demeanor. I am not sure how he tolerated being in my presence with the language I used in ordinary conversations.

One evening, there was a knock at my side door. Friends and family knew to always use the side door. I was not expecting company, and I never appreciated drop by visitors. I arrogantly opened the door. Much to my surprise, Keith was standing there with his nice, big, gentle smile. I, on the other hand, asked him with expletives what he was doing at my house at 7 p.m. without being invited. He simply said, "The Lord told me to bring you this book." He tried to hand me a book, and I recoiled. I said, "I am about to watch a television show, and if you want to give me anything, you need to come back in an hour!" I rudely slammed the door in his face. After all, there was a nighttime soap opera coming on, and it was much more important than anything he had to say. It did not matter to me that he drove almost an hour to get to my house.

I was quite certain, as well as hopeful, that my rudeness caused him just to leave. I was wrong. Exactly an hour later, there came the knock. Even more irritated this time, I opened the door, and there was that same smile once again. I'm sure I must have rolled my eyes, but I let him come inside. He resumed with "The Lord told me to bring you this book," as he reached out to hand the book to me for a second time.

The book was called *The Be Happy Attitudes* by Robert Schuller. I said, "What makes you think I am not happy?!" Well, to be perfectly honest, I did not quite say it like that. There were some explosive words in that question. He said, "All I know is the Lord told me to bring it to you." I refused to touch the book, so he said, "I will just leave it on your countertop. Have a blessed night." He saw himself out, and I stood there in shock.

The rage inside of me was at an all-time high. Who in their right mind would think that I was not happy? How dare he come to my house and presume such a thing! Oh, and to say, "The Lord told me to bring you this book", was the most ridiculous thing I had ever heard. In my seriously bitter mind, there was no way that God Himself would even think of me much less care enough to speak to someone else about me. I must admit that even through the rage, I felt something deep within begin to churn. I just did not know what it was at the time. I later realized that the Lord was trying to get my attention.

That book sat on the countertop for a week. As I cleaned the kitchen every day, I wiped around the book because I would not dare touch it. Then one night, when my husband and two sons were asleep, I was drawn to the book. I looked at it for a while then came up with a plan. I could turn off all the lights in the kitchen and living room because both rooms were connected. If I sat by the window, I could let the streetlight illuminate a few sentences at a time. My pride would not be able to handle it if my husband or children saw me with that book in my hands.

I did exactly as I planned and strategically sat myself on the sofa directly in front of the window. I very carefully opened only one of the strips on the blinds. If anyone walked into the room, I could drop the book beside me, and they would never know.

As I began to read, I was taken in by the storyline. The feelings that were stirring within me were so strong that I did not want to put the book down- the same book that I refused even to touch for the past week! Somewhere around page forty, there was a prayer giving the reader an opportunity to invite Jesus into their heart. I put the book down and said, "God, if you are real like this book says you are, then hold my hand right now." I was attempting to prove that there was no way the God in that book was real and personal or that He actually cared about me. Deep down inside, I was hoping I was wrong, because I didn't want what I was feeling to end.

I fully extended my right arm up in the air with my eyes closed, not even realizing that this is a sign of surrender. In a moment, there was an incredibly strong yet comforting grip on my forearm. I never once opened my eyes, not because I was afraid, but because I had never in my life felt such peace- instant peace. I then gripped onto the forearm of the One who was holding mine.

I cannot tell you everything that happened during this time because it was so supernatural there are no words to describe it. I can only say it felt like a purging was taking place- a gentle pulling out of the anger, rage, bitterness, and hatred that was inside of me. It was almost as if a plug was pulled out of a drain and everything was able to begin flowing. There was no struggle, no pain, not even an ounce of condemnation. I felt pure, unconditional love that I didn't have to ask or beg for. There was what seemed like an open fountain washing over me from heaven and pouring into every fiber of my being.

I can remember my mother putting drawing salve on a splinter when I was a little girl. Drawing salve pulls out the foreign matter without having to dig it out painfully. What I was experiencing was the Holy Spirit drawing all those things out of me while infusing me with the love and peace of the Most-High God- a love and peace that I never knew existed. It was such a great exchange!

God met me right where I was and stayed with me in that spot on my sofa for five hours. He did not require that I ask for forgiveness or even repent before He showed up. He simply came and covered me in love while in my horribly sinful state. The only requirement was an invitation from me.

As He poured His love into me that night, a repentant heart was born. My hardened heart was made compassionate. It was five glorious hours with the King of Kings and Lord of Lords. My life has never been the same again. Hallelujah!

The sun began to peek through the windows all throughout my house, and I was aware of myself again. However, this time I was light-hearted. I was happy. I felt love- real, true, and genuine love for the first time in my life. The colors all around me even seemed more vibrant.

I heard my husband getting out of bed, and I hurried to greet him. He went into the office every morning before work. For probably the first time ever, I made lunch for him to take to work. I wrote him a note on the dry erase board in our home office asking him to forgive me for being so hateful all those years. I knew he read my note, but he came out of the room emotionless. He was a very kind and gentle man, so this was unusual for him. He left for work that morning without kissing me goodbye, which he had never done before. He did not even take the lunch that I made for him.

What I experienced that night was nothing short of a miracle. I truly had the joy of the Lord. I knew beyond a shadow of a doubt that I was somehow loved by the Creator of all things. I was no longer an angry and bitter woman. In fact, without even realizing it, the foul language left me and has never come back.

My husband told me a few days later that whatever phase I was going through would end, and I would be hateful again. I could understand why he would think that way. The change in me seemed too good to be true.

When I was reading the book, it said to tell someone that you are now born again. I figured the best person to tell was my next-door neighbor. She was the secretary for a Christian church in our community. I only knew that because she parked the church van in her driveway next to my front door every day.

Remember, I had a very foul mouth and did not care who heard it. Imagine her surprise when I knocked on her door and said, "Hi, I'm Cheryl, your next-door neighbor (as if she didn't know that), and I gave my life to Jesus." She said, "Well, praise the Lord!" I asked if I could go to her church, and she was elated. She proceeded to hand me a few small Christian tracks, and I gratefully accepted them. I wanted to read everything I could get my hands on.

The supernatural experience I had just gone through with the Lord brought me back to two previous encounters that I had with Him. I remembered being very young and feeling so alone even though I lived in a house filled with my family. As I was lying in bed, the overwhelming feeling of being unloved gripped me. I even felt extremely dizzy. In the darkness of my bedroom, I raised my right arm toward the ceiling, and I said, "God, please hold my hand until I go to sleep." The next morning, when I woke up, my arm was still raised, and that terrible feeling was gone.

One year after my first son was born, I went to Cosmetology school. Although my ex-husband and I were only sixteen and nineteen when we got married, we had our finances in order. My older sister Terry was instrumental in teaching me how to budget, which I am forever grateful for. We planned to have our second baby when I was nineteen.

In the first trimester of my second pregnancy, I was working for a man who owned a hair salon in New Orleans. He was a born-again Christian, which was something I knew nothing about at that time. This led to my second experience with the Lord.

One day while I was at work, I started feeling very sick, but not sick from pregnancy. I was burning up with fever and developed a sore throat and body aches. He said, "Do you want to be healed?" I was so miserable that I said, "Of course I do!" He told me to sit in his chair and explained that he was going to anoint me with oil and pray over me. It seemed strange, but I was willing to try anything. He sounded so confident, and I had nothing to lose. He did exactly as he said. A minute after he started praying, the fever broke. I was soaking wet with sweat, the sore throat went away, and my body aches disappeared! He told me to take off early and go home and rest.

Before leaving the hair salon, he gave me the numbers on the car radio for a Christian radio station to listen to on the way home. I listened to it for about a week, and sadly, life went back to the way it had always been. It amazes me how the Lord was with me all those years, waiting patiently for my surrender. I am so glad He never gave up on me.

CHAPTER TWO
SHOCKING TRUTHS

About a week after I gave my life to Christ, I discovered that my husband had been unfaithful. The affair had been going on for about a year when I found out. As is often the case, it was a person with whom I was extremely close.

The way I found out about the affair was a bit strange. I was standing at the same countertop where the book was. As I was going through some mail, my husband walked in from work. I greeted him, and he was just as rude as he was the day that I received Christ. In fact, the whole week had been like that. He even stopped kissing me hello or goodbye. I told him, "I love you," and he responded, "But I don't love you anymore." Without a second thought, I said, "I know you love *Tonya*, but I love you enough for both of us." He ran to the room and locked the door behind him. I found out later that he hid the gun that we had in the closet because the old person that I was, in a bitter rage, was quite capable of doing something I would regret later.

As he ran into the room, a warmth came over me. I felt peace surrounding me just like the night when the Lord was with me for five hours on my sofa.

Although her name came out of my mouth, I can tell you that I had no clue that she and my husband were having a relationship prior to speaking her name. The sting of this reality was sharp, but the comfort I felt from God at the same moment was even greater. The Lord was covering me in His peace the entire time.

Please do not misunderstand what I am about to say. There is never an excuse for adultery, but I can tell you that I played a big part in his straying by the way I treated him prior to salvation. I repented and apologized for the years that I demeaned him verbally. It took quite a while for him to repent of the unfaithfulness. There were times that he would tell me how much he missed *Tonya* and wanted to be with her. *Tonya* ended the relationship with him when it was exposed because she wanted her own marriage to work. This crushed him as much as his unfaithfulness did to me. The difference for me was that now I had the Lord to carry me through the pain.

My actions and attitude after the affair was exposed were completely opposite of who I was before. I extended kindness and love to my husband regardless of his withdrawal from me. Eventually, he did repent, and we moved on from there. He later told me that it was the real change in me that caused him to want to pursue a relationship with the Lord as well. He started coming to church and got involved in ministry shortly after. Life seemed to be going well, at least for a while.

There were several more affairs throughout our marriage of thirty-two years. I never understood how someone could do the same things repeatedly, especially a Christian who repented and cried out to God after each time. Many years later, the Lord clearly showed me how wounds in his soul caused all of it. We all have wounds in our souls and deal with them on different levels. I will expound on soul wounds in the pages to come.

I can only say that it was the grace of God that my ex-husband did cry out each time and that I was willing to forgive. There were many great years in between each incident, but in the back of my mind, I was always afraid of there being a next time. Usually each "next time" was every six to seven years.

The final act of adultery in our marriage was exposed to me through the Lord while I was sleeping. I was laying on my right side, and there was a gentle tapping on the front of my left shoulder. I expected to open my eyes and see one of our triplets trying to wake me up. Much to my surprise, when I opened my eyes, there was a large silhouette standing before me. A soft voice said, "Confront him now. He is having another full-fledged affair."

The deepest pain hit my gut. I quickly sat up and shook him awake. Through tears of anguish, I said, "The Lord just told me you are having another affair!" He sat up, held me, and said, "No, you just had a bad dream." He reassured me that it was not true. I turned over and laid back down. It could not have been more than a minute later when the gentle tapping happened once again. When I opened my eyes this time, I was told, "Tell him either he is a liar, or the Holy Spirit is a liar. Which one is it?"

When I sat up that time, I blurted out the words I was told, and he immediately jumped out of bed knowing he was exposed once again. This time, however, he did not cry out, and he did not repent. Instead, he took his belongings and left to be with his new lover. This took place three days after we celebrated our thirty- second wedding anniversary.

My world seemed to have crashed around me. My husband and I had ten-year old triplets at home, and they were very close to him. The whirlwind of devastation is inexplicable. Our grown children and our grandchildren were equally devastated. I had never been angry with the Lord through any of the affairs. This time, I did question Him though. I asked, "Lord, why would you let him leave me after I have forgiven him so many times?" The Lord clearly spoke to me and said, "He did not leave you. I took him away, lest you could never fulfill the destiny I have for you."

That was quite a response from the Lord. It did not sink in right away. At the time, I had no inkling that I would be called into the mission fields of the world.

There was a period of about four months that I felt like I was breathing sand into my lungs instead of air. You see, all the previous affairs were kept private. I shared them with my pastor and counselor only, and no one else ever knew- not my children, my family, or even my closest friends. I covered my husband's sin. I did not expose him this time either. Now the world would know because he left our marriage and exposed himself.

As business owners and Deacons in our church, most of our community knew us. They thought we had the perfect marriage. I was embarrassed and humiliated, but I had to lean on the Lord. My body went into starvation mode. I could not eat or sleep, but I could certainly pray. Sometimes, my prayers were just tears, unending tears. My pastor often said that tears are liquid prayers, and the Lord bottles all of them up.

So much happened in such a small amount of time that showed the greatness of God even in my worst heartache. I was surrounded by a small group of people who were my strength and encouragement. Let me stress that again. It was a *small* group of people. I did not share details with anyone outside of my group, nor did I seek an ear just to hear me out. The people surrounding me were there to love me, encourage me, carry me, and cover me in prayer. When they felt like I was going off the deep end, they were there to lift me up and even correct me. They know who they are, and I am forever grateful.

Through much prayer, my first husband and I were able to co-parent our children who were still in the home. It took about seven months to get to that point, but we got there. My current husband Paul and my ex-husband have a good relationship. For holidays and special occasions, we are all able to be together with our children and grandchildren. Only the Lord can orchestrate something like that.

I could have gotten caught up in my feelings of betrayal. However, I refused to allow unforgiveness and bitterness to destroy whatever the Lord had planned for my life after the divorce. It was not easy, but sincere forgiveness was a choice that changed my life forever.

In the natural realm, it would be practically impossible to have a thirty-two-year marriage end and still be able to get along. I admit that it is unusual indeed, and not many people could do it. When the Lord released me from the marriage, I was released completely of all romantic feelings for my ex-husband. He will always be the father to my children and the grandfather to my grandchildren. Never let anyone make you feel guilty or dirty for walking in the forgiving love of Christ. Our children and grandchildren have seen the true love of Christ extended in the worst of circumstances.

I will share another thing that I did that many have said and many more will say was crazy. Each one of the women my ex-husband had an affair with had serious inner struggles of their own. In fact, the affairs started with him "trying to help them," a ploy of the devil himself.

In my own heartache and pain, I chose to minister the love of Christ and the salvation message to each one of his lovers. One might ask, "Why would you do that?" My answer is that Jesus loved me so much that He sent His only begotten Son to die for me. The Lord loved me in my sin, and He loved those women in their sin too. I may not have been an adulterer, but I was a vile, mean, and bitter woman. Sin is sin, and He died for it all.

I must admit, the final affair that ended the marriage was a bit different. I did not minister to her at first; the thought of her was too unbearable. But several months later, she was diagnosed with cancer, and I knew that I had to reach out. Reaching out to her expedited my own healing. I went and prayed with her, and she is alive and well today.

Approximately a year later, she had a grandson born with a very small portion of his brain. He was not expected to ever leave the hospital. I knew that I had to reach out once again. Out of obedience to the Lord, I made an appointment with the family. I was allowed, even welcomed with open arms, to minister to them and pray over the baby. It is by the grace of God that he is also alive today although he has many challenges. I was even blessed to babysit him a time or two.

Chapter Three

DESPERATE MEASURES

With every affair my ex-husband had, my self-worth dwindled more and more. I had gone to the extremes trying to make myself look better for him. My thinking was, "Maybe if I was thinner or prettier he would not stray. If we were intimate more times per week, he wouldn't go to someone else."

I was always an average weight, usually wearing size eight pants, but after the third affair, I convinced myself that I needed liposuction and a tummy tuck. Many thousands of dollars later, puncture wounds all over my body, and a lot of pain, the doctor only suctioned out about a pound and a half of fat. The tummy tuck basically tightened my abdominal muscles, and there was less than an inch of skin to be cut from my stomach. My vertical C-section scar that went up to my belly button is now barely an inch lower than my belly button. In my own mind, I thought I was so big that the entire scar would be cut away, and I would have a beautiful unscarred stomach. I also felt like the skin on my eyelids was too heavy, so I had eyelid surgery too.

I was desperate to be genuinely loved as my ex-husband's one and only when all along, I was not the problem. He had many skeletons in his closet as the world would say. His struggles were from some deep inner wounds in his soul that were formed in his youth. It was the open door caused by someone else who took advantage. This led him to struggle with unfaithfulness.

The devil knows our weaknesses, and he will always tempt us with the same thing over and over. He never tries anything new because he knows what will bring us down in a moment of weakness. He waits for the opportune time to pounce once again. Most people do not understand why they feel the way they do and why they are driven to do the things they do. Everyone's experiences are different, and there is healing available for every hurting soul.

Once my thirty-two-year marriage ended, I was no longer driven to do everything I could think of to keep my husband. Now, I had to focus on myself and what I could do to find the deep inner healing that I so desperately needed. The revelations I will be sharing were revealed through the pain I went through in my life.

As long as I can remember, I had an addiction. It was not the typical addiction, though. One might even call it an obsession instead, but it held me captive until eleven years ago. Not all addictions are with drugs, alcohol, sex, gambling etc. I was addicted or obsessed with the scale and tape measure. I literally got on the scale a minimum of three times a day making sure that I wore certain articles of clothing that would weigh the same each time. I measured myself twice a day- arms, thighs, calves, waist, hips, abdomen, directly over my belly button and then one inch below, the center of my butt, and directly below it. I kept a log, and I compared the measurements constantly. If there was an increase, I would panic and starve myself until the extra weight came off.

For all my pregnancies, I scarcely gained weight. I gained only eleven pounds with my first pregnancy. When I left the hospital, I was twenty-eight pounds lighter. For my second pregnancy, I gained thirteen pounds, and for my third pregnancy, I gained sixteen pounds. I lived on a calorie restricted diet my entire life, and pregnancy was no different. That was certainly not healthy. It was dangerous!

I did not realize until eleven years ago that an incident in my childhood is what held me captive and caused the addiction/obsession, even mutilation at the hands of doctors. I came to know that this was not caused by the infidelity that I went through. Infidelity certainly fueled the problem but did not cause it.

When I was a child, we ate at my grandparents' home every Sunday. I have a big Italian family, so the house was always full of aunts, uncles, and cousins. One day, my grandmother called everyone to her attention, so she could make an announcement. She had a large serving fork and a large serving spoon in her hands. She tapped them together and said, "This is for the hog." She walked over to me and put the utensils in front of my plate. I love Italian food. But I also love salad and vegetables, so I wanted a little bit of everything. Evidently in her eyes, this qualified me as a hog.

Some people laughed, but my aunt, uncle, and cousin defended me. They were a great comfort to me, not only on that day, but throughout my entire life. They loved me and always treated me with kindness.

I had never been overweight by more than five pounds, until I reached my early fifties, and my hormones decided I needed an extra fifteen pounds. Thank God I received a deep healing before the weight gain because fifteen pounds to me would have seemed like the end of the world. I know that sounds ridiculous, but addictions completely distort the truth. That act of cruelty from my grandmother put such a deep wound in me that my entire life was affected and held me captive to the scale, tape measure, and unhealthy dieting.

My grandmother got very sick and was sent home on her death bed. Someone needed to care for her during the day while my dad and uncles were at work, and my aunts needed help. I owned a hair salon at the time, so I decided to close temporarily until she passed so that I could help take care of her. The doctors had given her approximately two weeks to live. I knew in my heart that I needed to be there. I was able to minister the love of Christ to my grandmother until she took her last breath. I had long since been saved, and I had forgiven her many years before she got sick. In fact, I completely forgot about the incident until my cousin Gina reminded me.

Even after being reminded, I still did not realize this was the catalyst for my obsession. The wound it created inside of me was as strong as the day it formed. I was just unaware until eleven years ago that every thought, emotion, and action concerning my body was driven by it.

Once I learned the revelation I will share, I was not only able to walk in forgiveness that I had chosen many years prior, but now I could walk in freedom! Oh, don't get me wrong. I still get on the scale now and then just to check in on myself. As for a tape measure, it doesn't even cross my mind.

About a year ago, I found one of my old measure sheets, and the freedom I felt as I crumpled it up and threw it away was amazing! Many people may not have measurement sheets that help them judge themselves negatively like I did. Instead, they keep a record of the wrongs done to them and therefore judge others. Both hold people in bondage. Trust me when I say throw away the records. They are not worth keeping.

Chapter Four

CHANGING MY FOCUS

Although I was saved and very active in church for over twenty-five years, I had no clue that the wounds stemming from my childhood and throughout my adulthood had such a hold on me.

I went through life teaching and ministering healing to others without realizing the depth of healing I desperately needed for myself. There were walls set up around my heart and mindsets that I was unaware of that needed to be broken.

Choosing salvation and choosing to forgive were the two foundational things necessary to be healed. Since I already practiced those things, what else could there be? You will soon find the answer to that question just as I did. Just keep reading because your complete healing is at your fingertips. God's Word will guide you through, but it takes work and determination.

Too many people say, "Just give your life to Christ, and everything will be okay." That statement is grossly overused and inaccurate. Sure, giving your life to Christ means a brand-new start. However, it does not erase the things that happened to us nor does it right the wrongs that have been done. It certainly does not exempt anyone from terrible things happening in the future either. Jesus Himself told us that we would go through hard times, but He also reassured us that He has already won the battles for us.

John 16:33 states, "These things I have spoken unto you, that in me ye might have peace. In the world ye shall have tribulation: but be of good cheer; I have overcome the world."

While going through the tribulations, or should I say, train wrecks in my life, the thought of peace seemed impossible. I cannot lie and say, "Oh, I had perfect peace knowing that my world had just been turned upside down." No! I could not eat. I could not sleep. I could not even think sometimes. The thought of getting out of bed was excruciating at first. But what I could do was grab hold of the Word of God, and I am so glad that I did. Please don't think that I was able to sit and read for hours at a time. I would find one scripture that I could meditate on. Sometimes, it seemed like I would repeat it a thousand times in a day.

I have always been a person who journals. My journals are written to the Lord and hold the rawest parts of my being. Every tear and every emotion lie between those pages, but in those writings, great revelation came to me and then eventually peace- true, genuine peace. It is amazing to look back and see where I was and where God has brought me.

One of the scriptures that I would cling to and repeat until it resonated in every part of my being is:

Philippians 4:8 "Finally, brethren (Cheryl) **whatsoever things are true, whatsoever things are honest, whatsoever things are just, whatsoever things are pure, whatsoever things are lovely, whatsoever things are of good report. If there be any virtue, and if there be any praise, think on these things."** (Parentheses added)

At times, it took everything in me to think of even one thing described in that scripture. Eventually, I would find something good to think about like the day when my children were born. I would cause my mind to go through every moment of the experiences. Temporarily, my thoughts were pulled away from the heartache.

Another scripture that was instrumental in my life is found in Isaiah:

Isaiah 43:18-19 (NIV) "Forget the former things and do not dwell on the past, See, I am doing a new thing! Now it springs up; do you not perceive it? I am making a way in the desert and streams in the wasteland."

`I constantly reminded myself not to go back and dwell on the past. There was nothing I could do to change it. A person cannot drive from point A to point B while having their eyes fixed on the rearview mirror. The focus must be in front of us. I had to be determined to look for the 'new thing' that the Lord was doing. I can honestly say I couldn't imagine a "new thing" coming through the pain I was in. I would tell the Lord, "Your Word says that You are doing a new thing, so please bring it to me in spite of my lack of faith or vision in this trial."

This next scripture is one of my life verses. If you ever receive a card from me, you will always see this scripture written in it:

Psalm 37:4 "Delight yourself in the Lord and He will give you the desires of your heart."

Delighting in Him means spending time in His Word, in prayer, and in worship. By no means was I jumping up and down in happy bliss all the time. Delighting in Him was often just sitting in my quiet place, letting worship music consume me while tears were streaming from my eyes. The presence of God would fill the room with a peace that soothed my soul and settled me down. My desires eventually went from just trying to survive the pain to asking the Lord, "How can I serve You through the pain?" I've learned that serving others in the depth of my despair causes great turmoil to the devil. That's the only turmoil I want to cause!

There were many other scriptures that were lifesaving verses for me, but those three somehow pulled my thoughts back in from a very dark place.

Throughout my entire walk with Christ, I had a very small group of believers that I confided in and sought counsel from. I have many friends, but very few on whom I lean on in the horrifying times of my life.

However, against my better judgement, I leaned on someone in the last few years who was not part of my lifelong circle of Godly counsel. This was a fairly new believer in Christ, and we developed a friendship; I really trusted that person. I learned the hard way that not everyone is a true friend.

Sadly, I trusted her with my crushed heart after a devastating event occurred. An event that the Lord turned into an astounding blessing that led to my husband Paul's healing. His healing caused our ministry to propel. A little more than a year later, the event was twisted to bring ugly false accusations. The following scripture was in full motion in our lives.

Romans 8:28 "All things work together for the good of those who love God and are called according to His purpose."

Obviously, the "all things" in Romans 8:28 must be bad things or not so pleasant things because God would not have to turn things that are already good into good, right?

Keep your circle of support small, and let it be tried and true people in Christ whom you have known and trusted for a long time.

CHAPTER FIVE

DEEP WOUNDS AND GENERATIONAL CURSES

I've come to discover that even when things work out for the best, fear, anxiety, and a whole array of other feelings we experience do not just go away. They eventually sink into the recesses of our minds and can be triggered with any similar situation. Deep inner wounds dictate our thinking and they are often wounds that we do not even know are there.

The things that we dwell on in our minds will control our emotions, and our emotions will determine the actions we take. This vicious cycle will play out for the rest of our lives unless they are identified, acknowledged, and then healed.

What exactly are wounds in the soul, and where do they come from? Wounds come in several different ways, and some have nothing to do with you personally. We will explore the different ways of entry.

Generational curses are a common cause. They are passed down through our bloodlines.

> **Numbers 14:18 (ESV) states, "The Lord is slow to anger and abounding in steadfast love, and forgiving iniquity and transgression, but he will by no means clear the guilty, visiting the iniquity of the fathers on the children, to the third and fourth generation."**

God does not put curses on people to force them to serve Him. He gave each person a free will, and it is the will of the people to either serve the Lord or not. Their own choice to pursue evil is what brings the curses. Every generation that does not deal with the curses begins a new generation. This means that the cycle does not end after the original fourth generation because the curses that were passed down were not broken, therefore the behaviors and choices continue as do the curses.

The great news is that we, as Christians, have the power and the authority of the Lord Jesus Christ to break these curses! You will soon learn how to break them so that the following scriptures will become a reality in your life.

2 Corinthians 5:17 "Therefore if any man be in Christ, he is a new creature (creation)**: old things are passed away; behold, all things are become new."** (Parentheses added)

John 8:36 (NIV) "If the Son sets you free, you will be free indeed."

You will not only read these scriptures. You will learn how to become the new creation and how to be set free through the Blood, the Power, and the Authority of Christ once and for all. You will also learn how to break these generational curses off from yourself and your children and future generations.

Here are some examples of generational curses dealing with behaviors and mindsets. It is not an exhaustive list: alcohol, drugs, sex, anger, rage, violence, pornography, nicotine, physical, verbal and emotional abuse, infidelity, gambling and eating disorders. These things can be traced back in your lineage. The addiction did not originate where you are seeing it manifest.

Manipulation, control, operating in witchcraft and the occult are also generational curses. If you carefully search, you will find that these things were experienced to some degree in your lineage.

The same goes with sickness, disease, and mental illness. Your health care provider will always ask for a medical "Family History." They are looking for things that are "hereditary". It is nothing more than generational curses that were passed down in your bloodline. Things such as high blood pressure, high cholesterol, diabetes, cancer, heart problems, depression, and the list is endless.

Wounds are also caused by traumas that we have experienced in our lives such as the death of a loved one, a tragic loss of someone close to us, miscarriage, infertility, a bad accident, injuries, being the caregiver for a sick family member and putting your own life on hold, loss of a job, infidelity, abandonment, rejection, divorce or a bad breakup, financial ruin, broken dreams, and constant disappointments.

Wounds come from sins that were committed against us such as molestation, rape, physical, verbal, or emotional abuse, and false accusations. We had no control over any of those things. Another person's free will took advantage of us and caused painful wounds that can consume our lives.

There are also wounds that are caused due to our own sins. There is an old saying, "Hindsight is 20/20." If only we knew then what we know now, we probably would not have done some of the things that we did. Sin has a way of taking us further than we ever expected to go and costing us much more than we ever intended to pay. That payment is not always monetary.

As previously stated, these are not exhaustive lists. They are only examples of some of the most common causes of wounds. We now have a glimpse of how the wounds came, and next we will discover how to get healed.

Chapter Six
FORGIVENESS AND PEACE

The main requirement for having all your wounds healed is forgiveness. Satan knows that you cannot enter heaven without it. He is very crafty in his schemes to destroy the destiny of God's people. His final destiny is sealed; he will spend eternity in the lake of fire. His desire is to take as many people with him as possible.

Do not let the people who hurt you continue to have power over you through your unwillingness to forgive. They have probably moved on in their own lives, and you are the one left suffering. Another old saying goes something like this: "Unforgiveness is like drinking poison and expecting the other person to die." The poison of unforgiveness damages the one who is harboring it, not the one whom it is against. We don't literally want the other person to die. What we really want is a genuine apology. Forgive them anyway, and let the Lord set *you* free! That will put you on the first step of the journey to the freedom that lies ahead.

The choice to forgive is not easy. You will not "feel" like forgiving. The hurt will not instantly go away, and your mind will still go to the pain. Instead of dwelling on it, be determined to repeat many times over, "I choose to forgive (name the person)." It will get easier as time goes by.

It is especially hard to forgive those who will never apologize. Forgiveness is between you and God, not you and the other person. As you choose to lay it all down at the feet of Jesus, the heavy burden you have carried is taken from you and placed into the hands of the Lord.

Too many people think that choosing to forgive means that what was done to them is somehow considered okay. This cannot be further from the truth.

Forgiveness does not release the other person from being accountable to God. It also does not mean that the relationship must be restored or that you should contact that person to extend forgiveness.

Put simply, forgiving others releases you to be able to receive all that God has for you. Jesus tells us in The Lord's Prayer how we are to pray:

> **Matthew 6:12, 14-15 (NIV) "Forgive us our trespasses** *as we* **forgive those who trespass against us. For** *if* **you forgive other people when they sin against you, your heavenly Father will also forgive you.** *But if you do not* **forgive others their sins, your Father** *will not* **forgive your sins." (Italics added)**

> **2 Corinthians 2:9-11(NIV) Forgiveness for the sinner: "Another reason I wrote you was to see if you would stand the test and be** *obedient* **in everything. Anyone you forgive, I also forgive. And what I have forgiven— if there was anything to forgive—I have forgiven in the sight of Christ for your sake, in order that Satan might not outwit us. For we are not unaware of his schemes." (Italics added)**

Our forgiveness from God is contingent upon whether we forgive others. We must constantly evaluate ourselves to be sure that we are not holding any grudges. A grudge is un-forgiveness, too! We all want and need full forgiveness which means that we need to extend it so that we can receive it.

We can walk with the Lord, pray continuously, attend every church service, do good works, prophesy, teach His Word, and still not be forgiven when we withhold the same.

Forgiveness is not a choice. It is a command. God is limited in what He can do for us when we do not forgive. Unforgiveness is a sin, and our address in eternity is determined by our willingness to forgive.

I recently went through some awful false accusations that were sent to me in writing. There was no mistaking the viciousness of the content. The words were very hurtful. This came from someone I love very much and considered a friend. The accusations were coming from the condition of that person's heart. The intent was to justify their own actions, but it was crushing to my soul.

As I was about to respond in my own defense, the Lord stopped me and said, "A gentle answer turns away wrath. Let me be your defense." My flesh wanted to attack, but the Spirit of God required the opposite. Peace came over me when I obeyed. With that peace came an overwhelming assurance that the Lord was working it all out for my good because I chose to be obedient. I am experiencing first-hand God moving in my life because I chose to obey.

Do not think for a minute that the accusations do not pop up in my thoughts. I must be careful to throw them out quickly. I also had to determine myself never to read those horrible words again. Reading them would only give the devil another opportunity to have power over my emotions.

In fact, that letter named other people who would have been very hurt had they read it. I decided to delete the letter from my email because, I will not lie, the thought came to me to send it to the ones it implemented as well. I would have been as hurtful to others as the one who sent it to me had I done so. Nothing good would have come out of it. I chose to forgive, so deleting the letter was the right thing to do.

The biggest battleground is in our mind which we will talk about in a future chapter. Do not forget the portion of scripture in **2 Corinthians 2:11** where we are told that Satan wants to outwit us. The Lord has made us aware of his schemes through the Word of God. Therefore, we cannot stand before the Lord saying that we did not know better.

Unforgiveness is the biggest trap of the devil, and it gives birth to bitterness.

The root of bitterness brings us nothing but trouble and opens the door to destruction physically, emotionally, and spiritually. As we learn the Word of God, we can be guided and protected from the devil's schemes. Make a conscious effort to exercise **Psalm 4:23 "guard your heart** (and mind) **for everything you do flows from it."** (Parentheses added)

> **Hebrews 12:15 "Looking diligently lest any man fail of the grace of God; lest any root of bitterness springing up trouble you, and thereby many be defiled."**

Our bodies are fearfully and wonderfully made by God; according to **Psalm 139:14.** Every part of our being has been intricately designed to work together. Our eyebrows even have a purpose. The hair on our eyebrows not only shows our facial expressions; it was designed to catch sweat from going into the eyes.

> **Genesis 3:19 (NIV) "By the sweat of your brow you will eat your food until you return to the ground, since from it you were taken; for dust you are and to dust you will return."**

When we are engulfed in bitterness, everything in our bodies becomes unbalanced. Anger, anxiety, and envy reach an all-time high. Stress hormones are triggered, blood pressure rises, heart rate increases, and depression sets in. Our bodies become subject to sickness and disease. We find ourselves in a fight or flight mode, constantly in turmoil.

When breaking down the word disease, we get dis-ease. Everything about us is in dis-ease waiting for the bottom to fall out at any moment.

Proverbs 14:30 (NIV) states, "A heart at peace gives life to the body, but envy rots the bones."

With forgiveness comes rest and the assurance of peace from our Lord and Savior Jesus Christ. That heavy burden you have carried for so long can be laid down once and for all. The peace of God is available for all His people. Let these scriptures resonate in your mind. Grab hold of at least one of them and personalize it as a great source of hope:

1 Corinthians 14:33 (NLT) "For God is not a God of disorder but of peace, as in all the meetings of the God's holy people."

Prayer: Heavenly Father, I desire peace in my life. I ask you to guide me and direct me, so I can get my life in order. In Jesus Name, Amen

Matthew 11:28-30 "Come unto me, all ye that labour and are heavy laden, and I will give you rest. Take my yoke upon you and learn from me; for I am meek and lowly in heart: and ye shall find rest unto your souls (mind, will, and emotions)." (Parentheses added)

Prayer: Heavenly Father, I come to you with a heavy heart, and I lay it all down at Your feet. I ask You to comfort me and help me find rest for my soul. In Jesus Name, Amen.

John 14:27 (NKJV) "Peace I leave with you; my peace I give to you; not as the world gives do I give to you. Let not your heart (mind, will and emotions) **be troubled, neither let it be afraid."** (Parentheses added)

Prayer: Heavenly Father, I ask You to give me Your peace. Settle my troubled heart and take away my fear. In Jesus Name, Amen.

Philippians 4:6-7 "Be careful (anxious) **for nothing; but in everything by prayer and supplication with thanksgiving let your requests be made known unto God. And the peace of God, which passeth all understanding, shall keep your hearts and minds through Christ Jesus."** (Parentheses added)

Romans 16:20 (NIV) "And the God of peace shall bruise Satan under your feet shortly. The grace of our Lord Jesus Christ be with you. Amen."

Romans 5:1 "Therefore being justified by faith, we have peace with God through our Lord Jesus Christ:"

Psalm 29:11 "The LORD will give strength unto his people; the LORD will bless his people with peace."

1 Peter 5:7 "Casting all your care upon him; for He careth for you."

2 Thessalonians 3:16 "Now the Lord of peace himself give you peace always by all means. The Lord be with you all."

Isaiah 26:3 "Thou wilt keep him in perfect peace, whose mind is stayed on thee: because he trusteth in thee."

Colossians 3:15 "And let the peace of God rule in your hearts, to which also ye are called in one body; and be ye thankful."

I pray that these scriptures about peace will bring you comfort in your desperate times.

Chapter Seven

LAYING THE FOUNDATION

For those of you who have not yet decided to follow Christ, I pray that you find hope like never before. For brand new Christians, my prayer is that you become enlightened as God's Holy Word unfolds before your eyes. For those who have been serving God for years, I pray that you are taken to a whole new level of understanding in the same manner that I was.

I believe that through the revelations I am about to share, the love of Christ will consume you with such comfort and peace that can be found in no other way. May you come to know of what great value you are to the King of Kings and the Lord of Lords.

In my early walk with the Lord, I had no idea of the depth of God's provision for us. I knew of His love through the ultimate sacrifice of our Lord and Savior Jesus Christ on the cross. What I did not know was that provision means more than just monetary or material things. He loves us so much that through Christ, God provided complete and total healing for every part of our being: physically, emotionally, and spiritually.

The previous chapters were a prelude to the scriptural revelations that will lead you into a new realm of complete freedom that God has for His people.

When I first gave my life to Christ, I was told to start reading the Bible in the book of John. I had no prior knowledge of the Bible, and this was the first time I had ever read it. I took to this new reading very slowly and pondered every sentence.

Together, let's begin building a strong Scriptural foundation through the Word of God. We will be starting in reverse by going to the New Testament first in the Book of John. We will then go all the way back to the Old Testament Book of Genesis.

I am no English major, but when I started reading in John, I immediately noticed that in John 1:1 the word "*Word*" was capitalized, and I was intrigued by that. Then, verses 2-4 kept referring to "*him.*" Who could be the "*him*" that is being referred to? In certain translations, "*him*" was capitalized in the middle of a sentence.

> **John1:1-5 (NIV) says, "In the beginning was the Word, and the Word was with God, and the Word was God. The same was in the beginning with God. All things were made by him; and without him was not anything made that was made. In him was life; and the life was the light of men. And the light shineth in darkness; and the darkness comprehended it not."**

It wasn't until I reached John 1:14-18 that it all made sense. There was my answer, *Word* and *him* meant Jesus! For a new believer, this was an incredible discovery.

> **John 1:14-18 (NIV) "The Word became flesh and made his dwelling among us. We have seen his glory, the glory of the one and only Son, who came from the Father, full of grace and truth. No one has ever seen God, but the one and only Son, who is himself God and is in closest relationship with the Father, has made him known."**

I became very hungry for the Word of God, and He so graciously gave me clearer understanding in so many ways. The more I read the Bible, the more I wanted to read it.

One of my new Christian friends suggested that I buy a study Bible, so I did. I was amazed with the cross references. It took me a while to figure out how to use them, but once I learned, I went on a never-ending quest through the Word of God. The cross reference for John chapter 1 brought me to Genesis chapter 1.

> **Genesis 1:1-2 (NIV) "In the beginning God created the heavens and the earth. And the earth was without form, and void; and darkness was upon the face of the deep. And the Spirit of God moved upon the face of the waters."**

That portion of scripture said that God created the heavens and the earth. According to John 1:1-3 Jesus, the Word, was with God in the beginning, and all things were made by him. So, we can clearly see through Scripture that Jesus was always with the Father. I want that to be clear because some people, like me, who never had a foreknowledge of Scripture, have believed that Jesus did not exist until he was born of the Virgin Mary. We will look at John 1:3 once again:

> **John 1:3 "All things were made by him; and without him was not anything made that was made."**

Now, concerning the Holy Spirit, we read in Genesis chapter 1 that He was also there with God from the very beginning.

> **Genesis 1:2 "the Spirit of God moved upon the face of the waters."**

These scriptures confirm that The Trinity – Father, Son, and Holy Spirit- were always present. There is no mistaking this truth. Some of you may say this is not a new revelation, but for a new believer with no prior Biblical knowledge, these things were huge to me.

CHAPTER EIGHT
REVELATION OF THE BOWLS

Through the years, I have had many eye-opening experiences in God's Word. I love to teach and minister the Word of God to whomever will listen. It was more than twenty-five years after I was born again that I had the great revelation that I am writing about now. It has opened my understanding to a whole new realm, which is a realm that I believe will set many people free.

I am a visual person, and I like to teach with visuals. I will explain to you what the Lord showed me, literally, by using a set of bowls in my kitchen. I pray that you will be able to see in your mind what I am describing in words.

One day as I was putting my dishes away, I had a medium size bowl that was just washed. I went into the cabinet and took out the larger bowl that it fits into. I had to remove the small bowl from inside of the large one so the medium bowl would fit. The small one was then placed into the medium bowl, and they were put back into the cabinet.

As I was doing this, the Lord reminded me that He made man in His own image. My thought was, "What do these three bowls have to do with that?" As I pondered that thought, what came to me was that God the Father, the Son, and the Holy Spirit are three in one, which I already knew since the beginning of my walk with Him. Was He trying to show me the Trinity by using the bowls as an illustration?

I picked up my Bible and then went to Genesis. Chapters one and two tell of the creation story, so I figured that was a good place to search for what God was trying to show me.

Genesis 1:26a "And God said, Let us make man in our image, after our likeness…"

When reading that verse, my mind pictures "in our image" to mean bodily form. We know that Adam's physical body was created from the dust of the ground. We also know that Jesus came to us in the form of a man thousands of years later. It is only natural to visualize a body.

Genesis 1:26 was written long before Jesus took on bodily form. It was not adding up in my mind that "in our Image" literally meant our bodies. We know that God is Spirit, so how were we created in His image if this is not talking about a physical body?

After doing more research, I ran across an interesting Scripture in 1 Thessalonians chapter five. I have read this scripture countless times through the years, but suddenly there was a whole new perspective.

1 Thessalonians 5:23 "And the very God of peace sanctify you wholly; and I pray God your whole *spirit* and *soul* and *body* be preserved blameless until the coming of our Lord Jesus Christ." (Italic added)

This portion of Scripture says that we were created with three parts just as the Trinity is three persons in one. We have a body, a soul, and a spirit.

While praying for clarity, the Lord showed me the breakdown of each one. The bowls served the purpose of describing each individual part of our design.

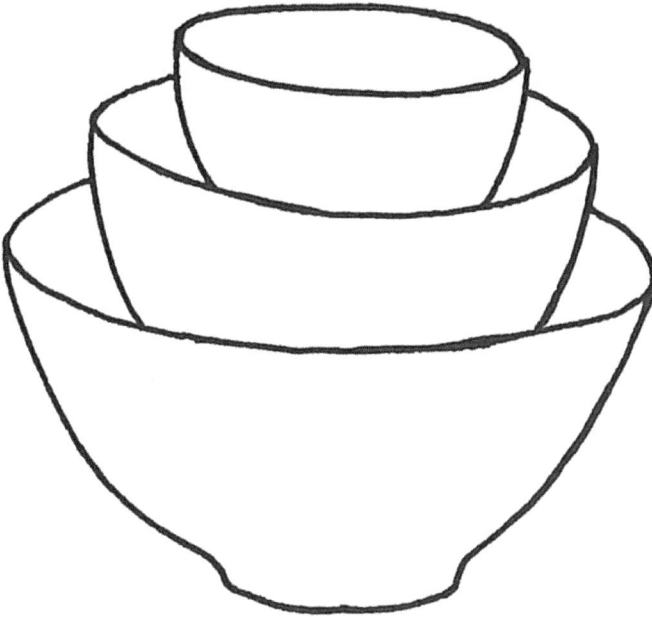

THE LARGE BOWL REPRESENTS THE BODY
WHICH HOUSES THE SOUL AND SPIRIT.

Genesis 2:7a "the Lord God formed the man from the dust of the earth."

Genesis 3:19b "...for dust you are and to dust you will return."

The body is the outer shell of each person, and it is a temporary part of our earthly design. Our natural body will not return to the Lord upon our death. Instead, it will return to dust. According to 1 Corinthians 15, we will one day have a glorified body, but not until the rapture of the church takes place.

1 Corinthians 15:42-44 "So also is the resurrection of the dead. It is sown in corruption; it is raised in incorruption: It is sown in dishonour; it is raised in glory:

it is sown in weakness; it is raised in power: It is sown a natural body; it is raised a spiritual body. There is a natural body, and there is a spiritual body."

1 Corinthians 15: 50-55 "Now this I say, brethren, that flesh and blood cannot inherit the kingdom of God; neither doth corruption inherit incorruption. Behold, I shew you a mystery; We shall not all sleep, but we shall all be changed, In a moment, in the twinkling of an eye, at the last trump: for the trumpet shall sound, and the dead shall be raised incorruptible, and we shall be changed. For this corruptible must put on incorruption, and this mortal *must* put on immortality. So when this corruptible shall have put on incorruption, and this mortal shall have put on immortality, then shall be brought to pass the saying that is written, Death is swallowed up in victory. O death, where *is* thy sting? O grave, where *is* thy victory?" (Italics Added)

Our natural body is what physically suffers with pain, sickness, disease, injuries, and death. According to 3 John 1:2, there is a connection between the body and the soul. If our soul is not well, it causes a breakdown in our body, which we will look at next.

THE MEDIUM SIZE BOWL REPRESENTS THE SOUL.

Genesis 2:7b "and (God) breathed into his nostrils the breath of life, and the man became a living soul." (Parentheses added)

The soul of man is what houses our mind, our free will, and our emotions. Thoughts are formed in our mind. Emotions reflect the condition of those thoughts. The choices that are made according to our free will are determined by both our thoughts and emotions, all of which are in the soul.

Soul is defined as- "the principle of life, feeling, thought, and actions in humans, regarded as a distinct entity separate from the body." (Dictionary.com).

In the definition of soul, we see "feeling" which is the *emotions,* "thought" which occurs in the *mind,* and "actions in humans" which is the free *will.*

Our soul is where the devil gains access. Let me say that again. Our soul, through our thoughts, is the only access point or "door" that the devil has. He plants anxious thoughts in our mind and is very patiently waiting for us to take the bait. Once we give him our attention, he consumes our minds and then enters our lives, leading us on the path of destruction.

II Corinthians 4:4 "The god of this world (Satan) **hath blinded the minds of them which believe not, lest the light of the glorious gospel Christ, who is the image of God, should shine unto them."** (Parentheses added)

Although II Corinthians 4:4 was written to unbelievers, Satan wants to blind the mind of believers of the power and truths in God's Word. When we have knowledge and understanding as God intended, we become a threat to the kingdom of darkness. Receiving Christ and believing His Word is only the beginning.

Hosea 4:6 "My people are destroyed for lack of knowledge:"

It is very important you understand that the devil cannot read your mind. The only ways the devil knows that he has your attention are by the words you speak and by the actions you take.

The Lord is the only one who knows the thoughts of man. As vile as our thoughts can be at times, He loves us anyway. Jesus never gives up on us, and He is always making intercession on our behalf.

> **Psalm 139:1-2; 23-24 "O lord, thou hast searched me, and known me. Thou knowest my downsitting and mine uprising, thou understandest my thought afar off. Search me, O God, and know my heart: try me, and know my thoughts: And see if there be any wicked way in me and lead me in the way everlasting."**

> **Psalm 94:11 "The LORD knoweth the thoughts of man, that they are vanity."**

The devil has waged war with our minds since the Garden of Eden. In Genesis chapter 3, we can see where the war against God's children began:

> **Genesis 3:1-5 "Now the serpent was more subtil than any beast of the field which the LORD God had made. And he said unto the woman, Yea, hath God said, Ye shall not eat of every tree of the garden? And the woman said unto the serpent, We may eat of the fruit of the trees of the garden: But of the fruit of the tree which is in the midst of the garden, God hath said, Ye shall not eat of it, neither shall ye touch it, lest ye die. And the serpent said unto the woman, Ye shall not surely die: For God doth know that in the day ye eat therof, then your eyes shall be opened, and ye shall be as gods, knowing good and evil."**

God did not say "neither shall ye touch it." Bring your attention to verse 1 and look at the word subtil. Subtil- "sly; artful; cunning; crafty; insinuating; deceitful; treacherous." (Webster's Dictionary).

In the New International Version, the word crafty is used in place of the word subtil. Crafty- "cunning; artful; skillful in devising and pursuing a scheme, by deceiving others, or by taking advantage of their ignorance; wily, sly, fraudulent." (Webster's Dictionary).

This was the devil's plan from the beginning. The serpent got into Eve's mind, planted deceitful thoughts, made insinuations, and then let her mind draw its own conclusions. Doubt was formed in her mind, and she made a conscious decision, an act of her own free will, that changed mankind forever.

The Word of God instructs us to take every thought captive so as not to get caught up in the trap of the devil, who is the enemy of our soul!

2 Corinthians 10:3-6 "For though we walk in the flesh, we do not war after the flesh: (For the weapons of our warfare are not carnal, but mighty through God to the pulling down of strong holds;) Casting down imaginations, and every high thing that exalteth itself against the knowledge of God, and bringing into captivity every thought to the obedience of Christ; And having in a readiness to revenge all disobedience, when your obedience is fulfilled."

Make no mistake about it. Our thoughts are taken captive regardless, either by us or by the enemy. If the enemy succeeds, we are brought down a very dark path of despair. Emotional instability, physical and mental illness, as well as actions that put our very lives in danger, evolve from our mindset.

The soul, which once again, includes the mind, will, and emotions of mankind, is the devil's target. He never tires of shooting his evil schemes with hope that he will hit the target in your soul and bring you to ruin. I will expound more on the soul in the next chapter.

THE SMALL BOWLS REPRESENTS THE SPIRIT

John 4:24 "God is a Spirit, and they that worship him must worship him in spirit and in truth."

James 2:26 "For as the body without the spirit is dead, so faith without works is dead also."

A born-again Spirit is required to enter the Kingdom of God. Our spirit is what is saved when we accept Jesus Christ as our Lord and Savior. Upon salvation, He sets His seal upon us according to 2 Corinthians 1:21-22.

The Spirit returns to the Lord:

Ecclesiastes 12:7b states… "the spirit returns to God who gave it."

The Lord receives our Spirit:

Acts 7:59 "And they stoned Stephen, calling upon God, and saying, 'Lord Jesus, receive my spirit'."

John 3:5-6 "Jesus answered, Verily, verily, I say unto thee, Except a man be born of water and of the Spirit, he cannot enter into the kingdom of God. That which is born of flesh is flesh; and that which is born of Spirit is spirit."

2 Corinthians 1:21-22 (NIV) "Now it is God who makes both us and you stand firm in Christ. He

anointed us, set his seal of ownership on us, and put his Spirit in our hearts as a deposit guaranteeing what is to come."

According to Scripture, our names are written in Heaven, in the Lamb's Book of Life. Once we have given our lives to Christ, and we have become born again,

Luke 10:20 (NIV) "However, do not rejoice that the spirits submit to you, but rejoice that your names are written in heaven."

Revelation 21:27 (NIV) "Nothing impure will ever enter it, nor will anyone who does what is shameful or deceitful, but only those whose names are written in the Lamb's book of life."

Satan is relentless in going after our thoughts (soul) to make us feel hopeless, defeated, and forgotten of God. The main goal of the devil is to have Christians reject Christ. An open door through denying Christ is the only way he has access to the spirit which is no longer sealed.

Isaiah 1:28(ESV) "But rebels and sinners shall be broken together, and those who forsake the LORD shall be consumed."

Hebrews 3:12-14 "Take heed, brethren, lest there be in any of you an evil heart of unbelief, in departing from the living God. But exhort one another daily, while it is called To day (today)**; lest any of you be hardened through the deceitfulness of sin. For we are made partakers of Christ, if we hold the beginning of our confidence stedfast unto the end;"** (Parentheses added)

Satan knows the scriptures, and they infuriate him. The only way to bring a Christian to hell is to get them to reject Christ. As much as Satan knows the scriptures, we need to know them, live by them, and cause him to tremble.

> **1 John 4:4 "Ye are of God, little children, and have overcome them: because greater is he that is in you, than he that is in the world."**

> **John 10:27-30 "My sheep hear my voice, and I know them, and they follow me. And I give unto them eternal life; and they shall never perish, neither shall any man pluck them out of my hand. My Father, which gave them me, is greater than all; and no man is able to pluck them out of my Father's hand. I and my Father are one."**

Chapter Nine

HEART AND SOUL

As Christians, we will always be targets for the devil. We need to understand that he cannot steal our salvation from the Lord. He can only infiltrate our minds and try to destroy our thinking, emotions, and then our actions. All of this is in the realm of our SOUL.

Since the devil knows that he cannot pluck us from the Lord (John 10:27-30), he works diligently to make us useless in building the Kingdom of God. I know many God-fearing people who live their lives overwhelmed by their emotions. They love the Lord but are paralyzed by the devil's tactics and are consumed in their own grief. Their bodies break down, and they live in depression. This is all according to the devil's plan for God's people. It is time to break out of that cave and be free!

With trials, temptations, and attacks, the devil wants us to walk away from Christ. His goal is to destroy our destiny in Christ Jesus through the opened door of our mind. If he cannot cause us to walk away from Christ, then his goal is to make us feel so hopeless that we walk away from our calling.

All generational curses, many that have remained dormant our entire lives, and the wounds that were discussed previously, lie in the recesses of our soul. These things are triggered by our thoughts. The more we entertain those thoughts, the more power the devil has over us.

Have you ever had a full-blown motion picture in your head of an incident or a conversation that didn't even happen? The scenarios of how you might react are endless. "Well, if this happens, I will do this, or I will say that." Our minds can surmise things, and believe me, these are never good things.

What's even worse is when an incident that did happen plays repeatedly in our heads to reiterate why we should stay angry and never forgive. All of this is the work of the devil to keep us from truly being free.

These thoughts will cause us to lose much needed sleep and to live in constant chaos. Anxiety creeps in, and we become a living, breathing mess. Once our minds become consumed by the devil's thoughts, we are then thrown into an emotional rollercoaster. We begin to get angry, resentful, and depressed, constantly complaining about everything and refusing to forgive.

Somehow, we can justify our feelings, and then we justify our actions. Our previously productive lives go around in circles, and we become stuck in the wilderness just like the Israelites, and therefore, never reach the Promised Land.

Unforgiveness becomes the breeding ground for bitterness, which is also the devil's goal. This then leads to our free will doing things that are not pleasing to the Lord or healthy to our bodies.

In a downward spiral that started in our minds, addictions are raised to life, and generational curses get resurrected. They are fueled by a powerful force of evil that was set in motion all the way back in the Garden of Eden.

The devil does not play fair. He has no boundaries and no age limits. He wants to destroy you through your thinking and cause you to live a defeated life. He only has the power that you allow him to have. As the scriptures unfold before your eyes, you will be equipped to take back everything that the enemy has stolen from you!

3 John 1:2 "Beloved, I wish above all things that thou mayest prosper and be in health, even as thy soul prospereth."

This scripture clearly says that our health, which is our body, and even our prosperity is dependent on the condition of our soul. Obviously, our soul determines our overall well-being.

By the time you finish this book, you will be equipped to have your soul set free. You will be able to begin walking in prosperity and in health physically, emotionally, and spiritually.

We will now look at some scriptures that talk about the heart. There is a direct correlation between the heart and the soul. Since our mind is what thinks and our soul houses our mind, will, and emotions, I believe it is safe to assume that the heart also refers to the soul according to the following scriptures. They speak of the actions or will of a person being either good or evil based on the condition of the heart.

It is our thoughts that determine how we feel. Our feelings are our emotions, and the way we feel emotionally determines our actions, which is known as our will.

Proverbs 23:7a "as he thinketh in his heart, so is he:" (We think with our mind, and our mind in is the soul.)

Luke 6:45 "A good man out of the good treasure of his heart bringeth forth that which is good; and an evil man out of the evil treasure of his heart bringeth forth that which is evil: for of the abundance of the heart his mouth speaketh." See also- Matthew 12:34b-35 (The condition of our thoughts and our emotions determines how we speak.)

Matthew 15:18 "But those things which proceed out of the mouth come forth from the heart; and they defile a man."

Psalm 19:14 "Let the words of my mouth, and the meditation of my heart, be acceptable in thy sight, O

Lord, my strength and my redeemer." (We meditate in our minds.)

Hebrews 4:12 "For the word of God is quick, and powerful, and sharper than any two-edged sword, piercing even to the dividing of soul and spirit, and of the joints and marrow, (body) **and is a discerner of the thoughts and intents of the heart."** (Parentheses added)

Every decision we make, whether good or evil, is from the depth of our soul. We must make it our mission to guard our soul, for that is where we strip the devil of his power over us.

Proverbs 3:5-8 "Trust in the LORD with all thine heart; and lean not unto thine own understanding (thinking). **In all thy ways acknowledge him,** (an act of our will) **and he shall direct your path. Be not wise in thine own eye: fear the LORD and depart from evil. It shall be health to thy naval and marrow to thy bones** (body)**."** (Parentheses added)

Proverbs 4:20-23 "My son, attend to my words; incline thine ear to my sayings. Let them not depart from thine eyes; keep them in the midst of thine heart (mind)**. For they are life unto those who find them, and health to all their flesh. Keep thy heart with all diligence, for out of it are the issues of life."** (Parentheses added)

Philippians 4:6-7 "Be careful (anxious) **for nothing; but in everything by prayer and supplication with thanksgiving let your requests be known unto God. And the peace of God, which passeth all understanding, shall**

guard your hearts (souls) **and minds through Christ Jesus."** (Parentheses added)

Psalm 51:10 "Create in me a clean heart, O God, and renew a right spirit within me."

Psalm 51:10 is such a powerful scripture when thinking of the correlation of heart and soul. My personal prayer is "Create in me a clean soul, O God and renew a right spirit within me."

Remember, all the wounds and generational curses are in our soul. As our soul is cleansed, we will truly be set free.

I will expound more about the devil's attack on our souls in the next chapter. I will also share with you how the enemy desires to physically kill us.

CHAPTER TEN

ISOLATION

The devil loves when Christians isolate themselves. Isolation gives him more room to operate in their thoughts. The battle ground is not in the natural; it is in the mind. It is imperative that we stay connected to the body of Christ. I can honestly say that I don't think I've missed church more than three times in any given year, except when out of town on vacation.

During what seemed to be the worst times of my life, I refused to stay isolated. I only missed one service during the final horrific ordeal that ended my thirty-two-year marriage, and that was the day after the shocking truth came out. I was in no way, shape, or form physically able to leave the safety of home with my ex-husband leaving.

We were Deacons in the church and part of the worship team. Both embarrassment and humiliation were at work against me. I had every excuse you can imagine, to stay behind closed doors. The Lord kept reminding me of how important it is for me to assemble with my brothers and sisters in Christ.

After missing that one service, my ten-year old triplets and I were there every time the Church doors were open. With the encouragement and love of my cousin Susan and her husband Mike, we made it to every service. Our church was approximately 40 miles away from home. I did not have the desire or the strength to drive, but they drove us to and from church for over six months. They were my Aaron and Hur, along with a few other people who carried me in prayer and counseling, through the biggest battle of my life. I never would have made it through the battle if I had allowed myself to be isolated. My grown children and grandchildren were instrumental in my healing by constantly coming to visit.

I cannot stress to you enough the importance of staying in the fellowship of the Church, regardless of the terrible circumstance you find yourself in. I could have watched sermons and worship services online. But in my desperate times of need, not one of those Pastors, Evangelists, or Worship Teams were coming to my rescue. I could not just pick up the phone and have them on the other line at any moment. I needed the Body of Christ even when I did not want to be around anyone.

I clearly remember the very moment that my ex-husband walked out of the door forever. It felt like my entire world crumbled around me. It was a Saturday morning. All my grown children came rushing to the house. My first request was to call my pastor. I desperately needed his voice of reason and his encouragement.

Unfortunately, he had just boarded a cruise ship and was leaving for seven days. I was able to talk to him for a few minutes before the ship set sail. He prayed with me, encouraged me, and assured me that the Lord knew what was happening and was with me through it all. Once he returned from the cruise, my pastor was a strong lifeline in the long battle I was facing.

All too often, believers will not reach out for help fearing that they will be judged, or even worse, told that there must be sin in their lives. The church must do a better job than that. It should be the place to run to for refuge and hope, not the place to avoid for fear of being judged. Just because a person is under attack or being tormented by the devil does not mean they have lost their salvation or that they are in sin.

When our bodies are sick, we can go to a doctor or a hospital. I am believing that through these revelations the Lord has given me, the body of Christ can be more equipped to minister to the deep wounds of the soul.

Having been in Christ for many years, I knew the Word of God was my only hope. Hebrews 10:23-25 told me exactly what I needed to do. I could have kicked and screamed. I could have stayed in isolation, but I knew that my spirit needed what my flesh dreaded- the fellowship of the brethren in the house of the Living God.

Hebrews 10:23-25 "Let us hold fast the profession of *our* faith without wavering; (for he *is* faithful that promised;) And let us consider one another to provoke unto love and to good works: Not forsaking the assembling of ourselves together, as the manner of some *is*; but exhorting *one another*: and so much the more, as ye see the day approaching."

I can assure you, ninety percent of my brothers and sisters in Christ stayed in the shadows. I am sure they did not want to overwhelm me. After all, what do you say to someone whose whole world just crumbled around them? (Or so it seemed at the time.) However, I knew they were praying for me and holding me up in prayer when I was too broken to do it on my own.

My mind played out every possible scenario to keep me home. "Everyone will be staring at me." "People are going to be talking behind my back." "I will get looks of pity." I had to make a conscious effort to be in church every time the doors were open.

Did I feel like being there? Absolutely not! It was a sacrifice indeed just to walk through the church doors. The song "We Bring the Sacrifice of Praise" by Kirk Dearman had a deeper meaning to me during this heartache. Facing my church family for the first time was very hard for me, but I am glad that I didn't delay going back. All the scenarios I had in my head did not happen. They graciously gave me space yet expressed love at the same time.

Every service for six months consisted of tears and grieving. My weight dwindled to an all-time low, but I was faithful in attending church. The brilliant light of humiliation and embarrassment that seemed to tower over my head started to get dimmer. I felt like I cried enough to fill my own river. My network of supporters was there to dry my tears and to lift me up. Isolation would have kept me broken for a much longer time.

CHAPTER ELEVEN
RENEWING YOUR MIND

So many Christians love the Lord with all their heart, but they are paralyzed by fear, anxiety, depression, and even shame. These things keep them isolated and affect the physical condition of their body as well. They do not walk about in the freedom that Christ has provided.

Some of the biggest attacks come to those who are making a big impact in the Kingdom of God. These attacks can cause even the strongest men and women of God to buckle under fear and anxiety.

Let us look at Elijah. His name means "Yahweh is my God." He was a powerful man of God- a prophet who heard God clearly. He walked in loyal obedience to the Lord. When given very hard messages to deliver, he did not cower away. He boldly did as he was instructed. Elijah hated evil, and he confronted it in obedience to God.

He experienced supernatural provision, supernatural protection, and many miracles. Elijah was a prayer warrior, yet he succumbed to fear when Jezebel, a most wicked woman who sought out and killed the prophets of God, sent a messenger to him.

1 Kings 19:2 "Then Jezebel sent a messenger unto Elijah, saying, So, let the gods do to me, and more also, if I make not thy life as the life of one of them by tomorrow about this time. And when he saw that, he arose, and went for his life, and came to Beersheba, which belongeth to Judah, and left his servant there.

> **But he himself went a day's journey into the wilderness and came and sat down under a juniper tree: and he requested for himself that he might die; and said, It is enough; now, O LORD, take away my life; for I am not better than my fathers."**

Fear will cause even the person with the strongest of faith to spiral out of control in their thinking. Elijah ran for his life, and he isolated himself. This gave the devil every opportunity to exaggerate the circumstances in his mind. It even caused Elijah to forget all that the Lord had done for him up to that point.

Fear brought depression and self-pity. Isolation meant there was no one there to reason with him and bring him the encouragement that he desperately needed. Elijah was physically exhausted, and he was an emotional wreck. His soul (*mind, will, and emotions)* was under great attack. The devil's goal was to cancel the God ordained assignments that Elijah was called to do and to destroy his destiny. But God did not abandon him.

> **I Kings 19:5-8 "There, under the Juniper tree, the Lord sent forth an angel to bring nourishment and rest to Elijah. And as he lay and slept under a juniper tree, behold, then an angel touched him, and said unto him, Arise and eat. And he looked, and behold, there was a cake baken** (baked) **on the coals, and a cruse of water at his head. And he did eat and drink and laid him down again. And the angel of the LORD came again the second time, and touched him, and said, Arise and eat because the journey is too great for thee. And he arose, and did eat and drink, and went in the strength of that meat forty days and forty nights unto Horeb the mount of God."** (Parentheses added)

The Lord, in His great mercy, came to Elijah and allowed him to rest and gave him provision. God himself met Elijah in the most trying time of his life. He encouraged him and gave him further instructions.

The Lord also gave Elijah a faithful friend named Elisha to whom he passed his mantle. We all need a friend like Elisha in our lives, one who loves us enough to reel us in when we have somehow lost our way on the journey. A faithful friend will not only correct us but will encourage us as well.

The entire nineteenth chapter of I Kings will give you the story of Elijah's fear and God's intervention. In II Kings chapter 9, the death of Jezebel took place as it was prophesied.

Elijah had to be rested and nourished for the long journey ahead, and it is imperative that we are as well. Our refreshment comes through the renewing of our minds. As we fill ourselves with The Word of God and rest in His presence, we are strengthened in the power of His might.

We renew our mind by reading, studying, and declaring the Scriptures over our lives. There were times that I could not concentrate long enough to read even one sentence. In those times, I would put worship music on and just sit quietly, usually with tears flowing. The Holy Spirit would fill the room, and a calmness settled around me. The presence of God was especially strong when I did not feel like sitting there, but I did it anyway.

Romans 12:2 (NIV) "Do not conform to the pattern of this world but be transformed by the renewing of your mind. Then you will be able to test and approve what God's will is—his good, pleasing and perfect will."

I had to renew my mind with the Word of God constantly. Taking my thoughts of despair and turning them heavenward was a challenge. It took great determination as I was living in the reality of what was happening around me. My finite mind did not have the capability on its own to look past the heartache.

In the beginning, every day was hard, and some days were worse than others. There were times when the thought of getting through one day seemed like it would be impossible. I had to focus on getting through one hour at a time.

It took my Infinite God and His promises in the Bible to nourish my soul. I slowly gained the strength to endure, and hope began overtaking the dread that I felt for so long. Victory was awaiting me on the other side. I just had to get there. Victory is waiting for you as well. Do not give up!

God's Word is powerful! Constantly recalling scriptures was most necessary during the night hours when there were no distractions keeping my mind occupied.

> **2 Corinthians 10:4-5 (NIV) "The weapons we fight with are not the weapons of the world. On the contrary, they have divine power to demolish strongholds. We demolish arguments and every pretension that sets itself up against the knowledge of God, and we take captive every thought to make it obedient to Christ."**

The more I would "take captive every thought to make it obedient to Christ," the less the thoughts would come. I eventually gained back the ability to sleep through the night.

Redirecting the painful thoughts was not easy. In fact, it was quite laborious, but it was worth the effort. Many miracles took place in my life and recalling them to my memory increased my faith in the current situation.

As you learn His Word, you will find freedom from the dreadful thoughts and hopelessness that seem to overtake you in trying times. It is very easy to get so caught up in the pain that you don't even realize when there is a shift toward the good. The Bible is full of instructions on how to get through every situation in life.

Hebrews 4:12 (NKJV) "For the Word of God is living and powerful, and sharper than any two-edged sword, piercing even to the division of soul and spirit, and of joints and marrow, and is a discerner of the thoughts and intents of the heart."

Colossians 3:1-2 (NIV) "Since then, you have been raised with Christ, set your hearts on things above, where Christ is, seated at the right hand of God. Set your minds on things above, not on earthly things."

Ephesians 6:11-12 (NIV) "Put on the full armor of God, so that you can take your stand against the devil's schemes. For our struggle is not against flesh and blood, but against the rulers, against the authorities, against the powers of this dark world and against the spiritual forces of evil in the heavenly realms."

Ephesians 4:22-24 (NIV) "You were taught, with regard to your former way of life, to put off your old self, which is being corrupted by its deceitful desires; to be made new in the attitude of your minds; and to put on the new self, created to be like God in true righteousness and holiness."

Oh, that word "attitude" really got me. I had my ten-year-old babies at home, so I had to work hard at not bleeding my pain onto them. In fact, they would sit with me every night and take turns praying out loud. They were not prayers of repetition but prayers from their heart. That was a bold move for three ten -year -olds. They were such an inspiration to me.

The depth of their prayers was that of adults who had been in Christ for years. They would plead the Blood of Jesus over the situation and ask the Holy Spirit to be with us. It was such sweetness in the most bitter of circumstances. They knew and would recite Scriptures to me, the same Scriptures I taught to them. Out of the mouth of babes came power and love.

As our minds are renewed by the Word of God, healing floods our souls.

CHAPTER TWELVE
OVERCOMING

The children of God are called to be overcomers. The Lord never promised us a life free of challenges. In fact, there are many scriptures telling us otherwise. God's Word, however, tells us the end of the story, and that end is victory in Christ Jesus.

To reach victory, we must do our part. I challenge you to research Scriptures on bad things that happen to good people. I could list many scriptures here for you, but it is always beneficial when we search the scriptures for ourselves. You will be delighted to see that the Lord has already provided a way for every situation in your life to be turned around for your good.

Romans 8:28 (NIV) "All things work together for the good of those that love God and are called according to His purpose."

As previously stated, if "All things" were already good, He would not have to make them work for our good. The Lord does not expect us to understand why things happen to us. He simply says to trust Him.

Isaiah 12:2 (NIV) "Surely God is my salvation; I will trust and not be afraid. The LORD, the LORD himself, is my strength and my defense; he has become my salvation."

If you proclaim Jesus as the Son of God and receive Him as your Savior, you can claim these Scriptures as your own. Hold onto them while going through the battle. They will help you to cross the finish line as an overcomer.

1 John 5:4-5 (NKJV) "For whatever is born of God overcomes the world; and this is the victory that has overcome the world—our faith. Who is the one who overcomes the world, but he who believes that Jesus is the Son of God?"

John 16:33 "These things I have spoken unto you, that in me ye might have peace. In the world ye shall have tribulation: but be of good cheer; I have overcome the world."

Revelation 12:11a "And they overcame him (the devil) **by the blood of the Lamb, and by the word of their testimony; and they loved not their lives unto the death."** (Parentheses added)

God has fully equipped us to be overcomers. The work was accomplished through the cross, and He never left us alone to carry on in life. Jesus promised us the Holy Spirit who is our teacher, trainer, comforter, counselor, helper, and advocate.

John 14:26 (Amp) "But the Helper (Comforter, Advocate, Intercessor—Counselor, Strengthener, Standby), the Holy Spirit, whom the Father will send in My name [in My place, to represent Me and act on My behalf], He will teach you all things. And He will help you remember everything that I have told you."

In my darkest hours, and there were many, I was desperate for comfort more than anything else. The Holy Spirit always met me right where I was at that moment. When I needed direction, He was there often sending me the advice that I needed to hear from someone who could be trusted. When I needed a defense against the enemy, He was my advocate. In the days of confusion and unrest, He brought me clarity. My part was simply allowing Him access into my despair.

Too many Christians keep the door to the darkest parts of their lives under lock and key, somehow thinking that it's too ugly, or shameful to allow the Lord into. He is our all-knowing God and sees it anyway. I am certain that it grieves the Lord to see His children suffering, but He is a gentle God and will not force His way into your circumstances. I want to encourage you today to invite Him into your pain, into your shame, disappointments, and despair. He loves you so very much and will sweep in with His unconditional love. The Lord desires to carry you through to the other side of your troubles.

When you finally surrender it all to Jesus, you will be a witness to Romans 8:28 and you experience Him turning your worst nightmare into good. It does not make sense in the natural realm, but He has done this for me time and time again. What He has done for me, He will do for you.

In Acts 10:34-35, Peter said that God is no respecter of persons for those who fear Him. His Word is true. Dare to invite Him into your circumstances today.

So many things that seemed to be worst case scenarios in my life were turned into blessings. Only the Lord can do such a thing. The things that looked like despair or destruction in my life, were always turned in my favor once I released it to Him.

The Lord is always with us, even in our loneliest times. If we allow Him access, the Holy Spirit will comfort us. Unfortunately, we focus on the pain of the situation and completely forget that we have the greatest counselor, comforter, and advocate within us.

John 14:16-17 "And I will pray the Father, and he shall give you another Comforter, that he may abide with you forever; *Even* the Spirit of truth; whom the world cannot receive, because it seeth him not, neither knoweth him: but ye know him; for he dwelleth with you and shall be in you. I will not leave you comfortless: I will come to you."

John 14:26-27 "But the Comforter, *which is* the Holy Ghost, whom the Father will send in my name, he shall teach you all things, and bring all things to your remembrance, whatsoever I have said unto you. Peace I leave with you, my peace I give unto you: not as the world giveth, give I unto you. Let not your heart be troubled, neither let it be afraid."

Jesus already empowered us to overcome every attack of the devil. I have found that many Christians are afraid to ask the Lord for miraculous things. They are afraid perhaps that He will not answer. Or even worse, that the answer will be the opposite of what they wanted. How then do we know if we do not ask?

As the Lay Ministers in Africa brought us through the many villages in Uganda to visit the sick, we noticed that they would bring an offering of maze flour or a few shillings (Ugandan money) to the sick person. They would visit for a little while and encourage them, but they never prayed with them.

After the first few visits, we asked the Lay Ministers why they weren't praying with the people. They said they don't pray with them because if God doesn't heal them, they will look bad. My husband Paul and I then stepped in and prayed for every person we visited. We explained to each person that we are not healers- only God can heal. We are just instruments for Him to use. The sick person was grateful to have us pray with them on the spot. The Lay Ministers observed and were encouraged to begin stepping outside of their comfort zone.

From that day on, many were healed, and the confidence of the Lay Ministers increased. We taught them about the power of prayer and about exercising their faith. They, in turn, taught others in their groups. Some healings took place instantly, and others happened after we left. The Lord's timing is always perfect.

Many times, we would walk along the village roads and run into people we prayed for weeks before. They were as good as new- broken bones completely mended with no medical intervention, ulcers gone, stroke victims fully recovered from paralysis, and many other healings.

Isaiah 55:8-9 "For my thoughts are not your thoughts, neither are your ways my ways, declares the Lord. For as the heavens are higher than the earth, so are my ways higher than your ways and my thoughts than your thoughts."

There was a precious little boy that we met the first morning after we arrived in 2020. His sister was carrying him on her back while walking through the Kitega Community Centre, which is our home in Uganda. He was about fifteen months old and was much smaller than other babies his age. We met his mother and saw them several times a week. I noticed that he cried a lot but never really thought much about it. Many Ugandan babies cry when they see Muzungu's (light skinned people), so I figured that was the case.

About five weeks later, after an extremely long day of ministering in a church service and then praying for people afterward, we got back to the Centre late in the evening. I was told that the baby boy died a few hours earlier. My heart was crushed. I said to our interpreter, "Bring me to him now!"

My two teenage daughters, another missionary from Scotland, and I were rushed over to the house in the village just outside the gates of the Centre. The baby was wrapped in grave clothes, and the entire village community was sitting outside of the house mourning with the family.

What I did next will seem a bit bizarre, but I had to follow the prompting of the Holy Spirit. I said, "Please give me the baby." They placed him in my arms, and after asking for permission to unwrap him, I did just that. I prayed for the Lord to raise him from the dead. I must have prayed and cried out to the Lord for twenty minutes. My daughters each prayed for him, and the missionary from Scotland prayed for him, too. He was not raised from the dead. He was rewrapped and laid back down on the mat. We all cried together for what seemed like hours.

I inquired of the Lord, "Why would you have me unwrap him and pray for him if You were not going to raise him up?" The Lord used the gentlest words with me as He said, "I Am the one who chooses to heal or not. You have been teaching the villagers and Lay Ministers to pray and leave the healing to Me. I had you practice what you preached."

What a tremendous learning experience. The Lay Ministers saw that I prayed confidently not knowing the outcome, and they have since been doing the same thing.

Unfortunately, his death was the result of complications from measles. His outward body healed, but the damage done on the inside destroyed his intestines. Healthcare and immunizations are not at their disposal as we have here in America and other parts of the world.

Some may say that the following Scriptures were not fulfilled with him, but in fact, they were. The Lord healed him on the other side. The lessons that were learned equipped the Lay Ministers to press on regardless, and countless people have been prayed for ever since. Many were healed instantly, while some were not, but all have been prayed for.

John 14:13-14 (NIV) "And I will do whatever you ask in my name, so that the Father may be glorified in the Son. You may ask me for anything in my name, and I will do it."

John 16:23-24 (NIV) "In that day you will no longer ask me anything. Very truly I tell you, my Father will give you whatever you ask in my name. Until now you have not asked for anything in my name. Ask and you will receive, and your joy will be complete."

Between language barriers or misunderstanding the interpretations, we had to rely heavily on the Lord for instructions on what to do and how to pray. When you find yourself in a situation, not knowing what to do, you can always ask the Lord for wisdom.

James 1:5-6 (NIV) "If any of you lacks wisdom, you should ask God, who gives generously to all without finding fault, and it will be given to you. But when you ask, you must believe and not doubt, because the one who doubts is like a wave of the sea, blown and tossed by the wind."

CHAPTER THIRTEEN
WISDOM TO KNOW THE DIFFERENCE

According to James 1:5-6, we should seek wisdom for every area of our lives, including job changes, relationships, finances, ministry, etc. My husband Paul had been doing missions work for about twenty-five years before we met in 2006. In fact, he came to my hometown as a missionary. He gave up his construction work in California, came as a volunteer for the rebuilding of my community after Hurricane Katrina, and he has never left.

Seven years after we met is when the Lord opened the door to a relationship for us. Never in all the previous years had there even been a second look at one another. We were a brother and sister in Christ, serving the Lord whole heartedly.

Prior to our marriage, I knew Paul was called to the mission field, not just as a missionary to serve, but as a ministry which would develop programs and trainings for people interested in missions. Leading and organizing mission trips is something neither of us knew anything about, but we were eager to learn. I gladly accepted the call as his wife and helpmate knowing that the Lord would have to guide us through every step. In 2018, we founded Samuel Worldwide Ministries, a non-profit, four years after we were married.

Paul knew that the first international mission's trip would be to Uganda. Well, this lily-white skin of mine gets sunburned quickly and the fact that my life consisted of air conditioning and the comforts of home, had me a little concerned. I began preparing myself in prayer and knew that we would only go when it was God's timing. I researched information on the climate and the culture, but no amount of information can prepare you for the realities that you face when you are there.

The first trip to Uganda did not happen quickly. We both embraced the call for our lives, and we knew that timing was crucial. The worst mistake a person can make is stepping out before the appointed time. The devil would love to make us think we are doing God's work while all along setting us up for destruction.

When a baby is born prematurely, they are underdeveloped and cannot sustain life on their own. Premature babies are at a greater risk of Cerebral Palsy, which causes weakness and loss of muscle control, making it hard to balance. Problems with posture, vision, hearing, speech, and intellectual disability are also associated with it.

Five of my six babies were born prematurely. Each of them had under development issues. I am thankful to God they did not have Cerebral Palsy. They had other issues, though. Some were worse than others. One of my babies had underdeveloped lungs and needed life support while the other four were on oxygen. All five of them had to be fed through a gavage tube because they did not have the ability to eat on their own. The part of the brain that tells them to suck, swallow, and breathe was not developed yet. We dealt with blood disorders, heart issues, intestinal issues, and many surgeries. My smallest baby fought death several times. Without intervention, all their outcomes would have been much different.

There were many other hurdles as well, all of which took time and great care to get through. Three of my babies had to have occupational and physical therapy just to learn to do the things that should come naturally. The therapy sessions were time consuming and went on for almost two years. If this process had been hurried or skipped, they would have struggled in those areas for the rest of their lives.

Looking at this from a spiritual perspective is quite interesting. Moving out before the appointed time will cause some of the same problems: spiritual weakness, hearing and vision problems in the spirit realm, and an unstable walk in the Lord. We will think that we are being led to move forward just because we have the desire. Desire is a great thing but going because we feel that we are supposed to go, and being sent by God are two totally different things.

We can make things happen on our own and convince ourselves that God opened the door. When we do that, His power and His protection is not with us. We go on our own strength, with our own abilities, with provision that we made happen. For what? To say, "I went in the mission field." Know the difference between going on a mission's trip because you want to and being sent by the Lord. Your very life depends on it.

Paul and I were married in 2014, but our first mission's trip to Uganda was in 2016. Although we knew the call on our lives, we also knew we could not rush things. The door to missions opened two years after we were married. It was about twenty-seven years after Paul was called to the mission field. He served God and proved himself faithful in local and domestic missions until the timing was right. I also diligently served in my church and community for twenty-five years prior to being sent out.

Even though I knew it was the right time, I needed the grace of God every moment. Mission trips in a third world country are not for the faint of heart no matter how big the desire. The travel itself is exhausting, not to mention the eight-hour time difference that we were entering. The luxury of resting for a few days to adjust is not afforded with time constraints involved in foreign missions.

II Corinthians 12:9 "And he said unto me, My grace is sufficient for thee: for my strength is made perfect in weakness."

There were two incidents on that first trip where our lives could have been in danger, but because we were "sent," the hand of God supernaturally protected us.

We have been invited as missionaries to several other countries, but we are not trying to build a resume of where we have gone and what we have done. We are simply following the direction of the Lord as we participate in building the Kingdom of God in the places and time frames that He sends us.

Please do not misunderstand me. Participating in an organized mission's trip through a ministry or organization is a great experience. I am talking about stepping out as a missionary on your own. Not everyone who goes on a mission's trip is a missionary. Being called as a missionary holds a great responsibility, and it comes with vicious attacks from the devil.

After our first trip in 2016, Paul almost died of a terrible fever. This was not a fever or a sickness he got while in Africa. It was six months later. Three hospitals and countless doctors could not find the cause and had no idea how to treat him for several weeks. They kept sending him home with 104 degrees temperature saying, "All of your blood work is normal. This is a Fever of Unknown Origin, FUO, and we cannot do anything for you." Those were the scariest words I had ever heard.

One night in particular, the Lord woke me up and said, "Pray over him now, or he will die!" Paul was sporadically breathing and would not respond to me as I was calling his name. I rebuked the spirit of death and commanded life back into his body for at least thirty minutes. Suddenly, he took a deep breath, made a raspy sound, and began to wake up.

I brought him to yet another hospital. This time an infectious disease doctor examined him and was determined to find the cause. He ordered blood tests that were not the ordinary ones done in an emergency room. He gave Paul a prescription for a "go-to medication" just in case it was bacterial.

The results came back several days later saying Paul had Brucellosis which is also known as Undulant fever. It is a vicious bacterial infection that is transmitted by contact with infected animals or infected meat from an animal. This is so rare and precisely why it was overlooked. It is easily treated IF it is diagnosed. If not, it is fatal.

The Center for Disease Control was calling my phone with so many questions like "Is Paul a butcher?" and "Did Paul eat any exotic meat right before the fever started?" There was no possible way that he was exposed to these bacteria, without me being exposed as well. The only explanation was that this was an all-out attack from the pit of hell.

Thank God the "go-to medication" was the antidote! The high fever broke within forty-eight hours and was finally able to be controlled. It took quite a few weeks after he started the medicine to be completely free of fever. He had to take the medication for almost two months and eventually started gaining back his strength.

Then there was the horrible incident five days before our mission's trip in 2019. Paul was taking a fifteen-hundred-pound manlift off his trailer. He was guiding the lift down the ramps and the weight shifted.

As I was backing out of the driveway, I saw my ninety-pound son flying in the air. I watched in what seemed like slow motion as this manlift was falling and my husband was going down with it. Paul could not get out of the way, but he saved our son's life by throwing him across the yard.

In complete shock, I jumped out of my vehicle and ran across the field. The manlift was on top of him. There was a plastic bucket barely holding up one corner of the machine; otherwise, he would have been instantly crushed to death. Our son got beneath the corner and lifted the machine enough for Paul to pull himself from under it. God gave them both supernatural strength, and He even used a plastic bucket that should have crumbled with that much weight falling on top of it.

As soon as Paul came out from under the manlift, he stood up, walked over to his trailer, and collapsed on his back. I have never heard such loud and heartbreaking screams as I did when he fell onto the trailer.

This was really happening but seemed surreal. I dialed 911, and the fire department was there in minutes. Paul was transported to University Hospital in New Orleans because they have the best trauma department in our city.

I was told, "This type of injury does not end well." One of his kidneys was damaged, one lung was filled with fluid, and nine ribs in his back were ripped apart. They were not clean breaks.

The doctor told me they were putting him in ICU once he was stabilized. The emergency room was flooded with family, friends, and our Pastor. Paul was prayed over; all we could do was wait and trust God to answer the prayers.

Once Paul was stabilized several hours later, the doctor came back and said, "The new scan shows that his lung is much better, and his kidney has improved as well." Instead of ICU, he was put in a room on the trauma floor. Unbelievably, thirty-six hours later, we were in the vehicle heading home. He was in severe pain. but the only treatment at this point was going to be rest and time so he could heal. That, my friends, is nothing short of a miracle!

Paul and I lead a Life Group on Fridays at the time, and we usually had about ten or more people attend. I got him home and settled in the recliner on Thursday afternoon, and he refused to let me cancel the group for the next day. In extreme pain and bound to the recliner, we had the group over, and he wouldn't have it any other way.

The orthopedic surgeon wanted to see Paul in ten days to see how many ribs he would have to surgically repair. He was also concerned about hematomas. When the doctor looked at his new scan, he was amazed. All of his ribs lined back up and were healing well. He was even more amazed that Paul never had any bruising at all. That was two more miracles in the books!

Our mission's trip was not cancelled, but we did reschedule for five months later. Another strange thing happened five days before we were leaving for the rescheduled trip to Uganda. I was rinsing my mouth after brushing my teeth, and I had a sharp pain in one of my top teeth. This was very unusual for me. In all my fifty-six years, I've only had a few pinhole cavities, which were filled. I have regular cleanings and ex-rays that are always excellent.

I got an emergency appointment and was told that I needed a root canal immediately. The new x-ray compared to the previous one was unbelievable. The dentist said for a tooth to get that bad it had to have been neglected for a few years, but she knew that was not the case.

A root canal is done in several steps, over a period of a few weeks. There was no way to get this done prior to leaving, but I certainly could not leave with my tooth in that condition. The dentist did a temporary fix to get me to Africa. We were going to be there for two months, and she could not guarantee that the temporary fix would last that long.

When I arrived in Uganda, I had the root canal. Yes, you heard that right. I had a root canal without all the specialty equipment and perks of America. The first visit took about four and a half hours. The dentist did a great job, and it was a fraction of the cost. However, I would not recommend anyone to go and just get a root canal in a foreign country. The dentist I went to was highly recommended by our Ugandan son David.

I did not tell you these things to scare you off from doing missions work. I simply told you these things because the life of a missionary can be quite taxing. As missionaries in Africa, Paul and I not only serve the people, but we also teach and preach the Gospel of Christ in remote villages that deal with extreme cases of wickedness. Empowering God's people to have victory over the devil is a great passion of ours, and it infuriates the kingdom of darkness. The devil could care less that we volunteer to serve; it is the specific teachings that make us targets.

Participating in mission trips is a great blessing. I highly recommend volunteering to serve in organized mission trips. The experience is life changing. The place we bring volunteers in Uganda is a perfect place for families with children and youth groups. It is a great learning mission trip and is both safe and rewarding. We can organize trips through Samuel Worldwide Ministries, for anyone that is interested in going to Uganda or Kenya.

I want to encourage you to find organizations in your own area where you can volunteer. There are local food banks and soup kitchens that would love to have your help. Living in the Greater New Orleans area, we volunteer at The New Orleans Mission and Giving Hope Food Pantry.

Chapter Fourteen
POWER IN THE BLOOD

All throughout scripture, we read about the shedding of blood for the atonement of sins. The Old Covenant consisted of the shedding of blood of an innocent animal. That blood became the sacrifice for the guilty people.

Leviticus 16 speaks of the Day of Atonement. The ritual called for the shedding of blood for the forgiveness of sin. Aaron, the high priest, had to first atone for his sin and that of his household with a blood sacrifice. After he and his family were atoned for, he could atone for the rebellion and sins of the Israelites. This had to be repeated annually.

> **Leviticus 17:11 "For the life of a creature is in the blood, and I have given it to you to make atonement for yourselves on the altar; it is the blood that makes atonement for one's life."**

> **Hebrews Chapter 9:1-10 "Then verily the first *covenant* had also ordinances of divine service, and a worldly sanctuary. For there was a tabernacle made; the first, wherein *was* the candlestick, and the table, and the shewbread; which is called the sanctuary. And after the second veil, the tabernacle which is called the Holiest of all; which had the golden censer, and the ark of the covenant overlaid roundabout with**

gold, wherein *was* the golden pot that had manna, and Aaron›s rod that budded, and the tables of the covenant; And over it the cherubim's of glory shadowing the mercy seat; of which we cannot now speak particularly. Now when these things were thus ordained, the priests went always into the first tabernacle, accomplishing the service *of God*. But into the second *went* the high priest alone once every year, not without blood, which he offered for himself, and *for* the errors of the people: The Holy Ghost this signifying, that the way into the holiest of all was not yet made manifest, while as the first tabernacle was yet standing: Which *was* a figure for the time then present, in which were offered both gifts and sacrifices, that could not make him that did the service perfect, as pertaining to the conscience; *Which stood* only in meats and drinks, and divers washings, and carnal ordinances, imposed *on them* until the time of reformation."

The New Covenant of Jesus' Blood has all power and authority. It only had to be shed once for all mankind.

Hebrews 9:11-28 "But Christ being come an high priest of good things to come, by a greater and more perfect tabernacle, not made with hands, that is to say, not of this building; Neither by the blood of goats and calves, but by his own blood he entered in once into the holy place, having obtained eternal redemption *for us*. For if the blood of bulls and of goats, and the ashes of an heifer sprinkling the unclean, sanctifieth to the purifying of the flesh: How much more shall the blood of Christ, who through the eternal Spirit offered himself without spot to God, purge

your conscience from dead works to serve the living God? And for this cause he is the mediator of the new testament, that by means of death, for the redemption of the transgressions *that were* under the first testament, they which are called might receive the promise of eternal inheritance. For where a testament *is*, there must also of necessity be the death of the testator. For a testament *is* of force after men are dead: otherwise, it is of no strength at all while the testator liveth. Whereupon neither the first *testament* was dedicated without blood. For when Moses had spoken every precept to all the people according to the law, he took the blood of calves and of goats, with water, and scarlet wool, and hyssop, and sprinkled both the book, and all the people, Saying, This *is* the blood of the testament which God hath enjoined unto you. Moreover he sprinkled with blood both the tabernacle, and all the vessels of the ministry. And almost all things are by the law purged with blood; and without shedding of blood is no remission. *It was* therefore necessary that the patterns of things in the heavens should be purified with these; but the heavenly things themselves with better sacrifices than these. For Christ is not entered into the holy places made with hands, *which are* the figures of the true; but into heaven itself, now to appear in the presence of God for us: Nor yet that he should offer himself often, as the high priest entereth into the holy place every year with blood of others; For then must he often have suffered since the foundation of the world: but now *once* in the end of the world hath he appeared to put away sin by the sacrifice of himself. And as it is appointed unto men once to die, but after this the judgment: So Christ was *once* offered to bear the sins of many; and unto them that look for him shall he appear the second time without sin unto salvation." (Italics added)

The blood of Jesus is just as alive, active, and powerful today as it was the day it was shed on Calvary. The blood of Jesus does the following:

Cleanses:

> Hebrews 9:14 "How much more shall the blood of Christ, who through the eternal Spirit offered himself without spot to God, purge your conscience from dead works to serve the living God?"

Forgives:

> Matthew 26:28 (NKJV) "For this is my blood of the new testament, which is shed for many for the remission of sins."

> Ephesians 1:7 (NIV) "In whom we have redemption through his blood, the forgiveness of sins, according to the riches of his grace;"

Makes Atonement:

> Leviticus 17:11 (NKJV) "For the life of the flesh *is* in the blood: and I have given it to you upon the altar to make an atonement for your souls: for it *is* the blood *that* maketh an atonement for the soul."

Sanctifies:

Sanctify- "to set apart to a sacred purpose or to a religious use: consecrate." (Merriam-Webster)

> **Hebrews 13:12 "Wherefore Jesus also, that he might sanctify the people with his own blood, suffered without the gate."**

Redeems:

> **1 Peter 1:18-19 "Forasmuch as ye know that ye were not redeemed with corruptible things, *as* silver and gold, from your vain conversation *received* by tradition from your fathers; But with the precious blood of Christ, as of a lamb without blemish and without spot:"**

Heals and Delivers:

> **1 Peter 2:24 "Who his own self bare our sins in his own body on the tree that we, being dead to sins, should live unto righteousness: by whose stripes ye were healed."**

> **Matthew 8: 16-17 "When the even** (evening) **was come, they brought unto him many that were possessed with devils: and he cast out the spirits with** *his* **word, and healed all that were sick: That it might be fulfilled which was spoken by Esaias** (Isaiah) **the prophet, saying, Himself took our infirmities, and bare** *our* **sicknesses."** (Parenthesis added)

Reconciles us to God:

> Colossians 1:19-21 "For it pleased *the Father* that in him should all fullness dwell; And, having made peace through the blood of his cross, by him to reconcile all things unto himself; by him, *I say*, whether *they be* things in earth, or things in heaven. And you, that were sometime alienated and enemies in *your* mind by wicked works, yet now hath he reconciled."

Justifies:

> Romans 3:23-26 "For all have sinned, and come short of the glory of God; Being justified freely by his grace through the redemption that is in Christ Jesus: Whom God hath set forth *to be* a propitiation through faith in his blood, to declare his righteousness for the remission of sins that are past, through the forbearance of God; To declare, *I say*, at this time his righteousness: that he might be just, and the justifier of him which believeth in Jesus."

> Romans 5:8-9 "But God commendeth his love toward us, in that, while we were yet sinners, Christ died for us. Much more then, being now justified by his blood, we shall be saved from wrath through him."

Overcomes the works of the Devil:

> Revelation 12:11(NKJV) "And they overcame him by the blood of the Lamb and by the word of their testimony, and they did not love their lives to the death."

Makes us Righteous:

2 Corinthians 5:21 "For he hath made him *to be* sin for us, who knew no sin; that we might be made the righteousness of God in him."

Speaks a Better Word:

Hebrews 12:24 (NIV) "And to Jesus the mediator of a new covenant, and to the sprinkled blood that speaks a better word than the blood of Abel." (Abel's blood cried out for justice, Jesus' blood cried out forgiveness.)

When we pray, we are to plead the blood of Jesus over our lives, our families, sickness, disease, finances, and circumstances. I will guide you through this process in an upcoming chapter.

CHAPTER FIFTEEN

DUNAMIS, MIRACLE WORKING POWER

The word dynamite comes from the word "Dunamis." Dynamite is a blasting explosive that is used in demolition and mining. Anything in a dynamite explosion is destroyed.

Jesus operated in Dunamis power, which is explosive, incredible spiritual power against all the works of the devil. Nothing could resist the Dunamis power of the Most-High God as Jesus walked about. We will look at scripture that describes Dunamis power at work.

Luke 8: 42b- 48 (NIV) "As Jesus was on His way, the crowds almost crushed Him. And a woman was there who had been subject to bleeding for twelve years. But no one could heal her. She came up behind him and touched the edge of his cloak, and immediately her bleeding stopped. "Who touched me?" Jesus asked. When they all denied it, Peter said, Master, the people are crowding and pressing against you. But Jesus said, someone touched me, I know that *power* has gone out from me. Then the woman, seeing that she could not go unnoticed, came trembling and fell at His feet. In the presence of all the people, she had been instantly

healed. Then He said to her, Daughter, your faith has healed you, go in peace." (Italics added)

The word "power" in this verse refers to the Dunamis, explosive, miracle working, resurrection power. The woman's faith put a demand on the power of the Most-High God. Jesus felt power leave Him and go into the woman. This same Dunamis power is within every born-again believer! Imagine the King of Kings and Lord of Lords releasing His power upon you. It is the same Power that God the Father used when He raised Christ from the dead.

There are many examples of His Dunamis power throughout the New Testament. It was Dunamis power that Jesus operated in to heal the sick and the lepers, open the blind eyes and deaf ears, raise the dead, cause the lame to walk again, and cast out devils. Through the scriptures, you will see that God gave that same power to each believer.

Luke 24:49 (NIV) "I am going to send you what my Father has promised; but stay in the city until you have been *clothed with power from on high.*" (Italics added)

John 14:12- (NKJV) "Most assuredly, I say to you, he who believes in Me, the works that I do he *will do* also; *and greater things than these he will do,* because I go to My Father." (Italics added)

Acts 1:8 (NKJV) "But you shall receive *power* when the Holy Spirit comes upon you; and you shall be witnesses to Me in Jerusalem, and in all Judea and Samaria, and to the ends of the earth." (Italics added)

How can we do the same things Jesus did and even greater things without His power? We are to be His witnesses by proclaiming His Word, teaching salvation, praying for the sick, casting out devils, and doing the things He has done. We can accomplish this because the same power that rose Jesus from the grave lives in us!

Ephesians 1:18-21(NIV) "I pray that the eyes of your heart may be enlightened in order that you may know the hope to which he has called you, the riches of his glorious inheritance in his holy people, and his incomparably great power for us who believe. *That power is the same as the mighty strength he exerted when he raised Christ from the dead and seated him at his right hand in the heavenly realms, far above all rule and authority, power and dominion, and every name that is invoked, not only in the present age but also in the one to come.*" (Italics added)

Romans 8:11(NLT) "The Spirit of God, who raised Jesus from the dead, lives in you. And just as God raised Christ from the dead, He will give life to your mortal bodies by this same Spirit living within you."

How do we receive this power? Upon salvation, the Lord deposited His Spirit and power within us. However, most people are unaware. We did not have to pray for it or labor to receive it. He freely placed it within us.

2 Corinthians 1:20-22 (NIV) "For no matter how many promises God has made, they are "Yes" in Christ. And so, through him the 'Amen' is spoken by us to the glory of God. Now it is God who makes both us and you stand firm in Christ. He anointed us, set his seal of ownership on us, and put his Spirit in our hearts as a deposit, guaranteeing what is to come."

The Lord NEVER breaks His promise! To understand the concept of God's power, we must first know His Word. In the scripture reference above, it says, "And so through him the 'Amen' is spoken by us to the glory of God."

Amen- "It is so; so be it." (Dictionary.com)

Once we acknowledge that His power is present within us, we can activate it in our lives and nurture it through reading the Word. Only then can we apply it to ourselves and to the lives of others.

As I was teaching throughout Uganda and Kenya about the power of God that has been given to each believer, my intention was to speak about situations that they are familiar with. I would then be able to show them the spiritual side in a way they could understand. I had to use the term "resurrection power" because in their native languages, there was no translation for the word Dunamis.

To give you an analogy of acknowledging God's power, I first need to give you some facts. I believe it will then make sense to you. This is in no way intended to make God look like a big Santa Claus. It was a way of showing the power of God by using familiar circumstances.

In Africa, there is no such thing as government assistance. If you are homeless, you are on your own, that is, until the Human Traffickers come in with promises of a better life. We all know what tragedies that leads to- sex and labor slavery, and even organ harvesting. If traffickers do not overtake the homeless, the common criminals do.

The women and children are raped and are taken advantage of in every possible way. If you have no food, you starve to death. There is no free education in Africa, so if you do not have money for school fees or if no one sponsors you, you remain illiterate.

Witch doctors are everywhere in the villages, and they place curses on the people and on the land. Curses are very real, and people are destroyed by them. Curses of sickness, disease, poverty, addictions, and abuse are rampant. The villagers feel totally hopeless against these terrible forces of evil as they experience the reality of the curses in their lives.

Trust me when I say Paul and I have seen these things with our own eyes, and we have had the privilege of breaking these curses through what is being taught here.

I used the following analogy when teaching in their churches and villages:

You and your family are hungry, and you have no shillings to buy food. Perhaps sickness has hit your family members, and you cannot buy the medication that will easily cure them. You have no shillings for school fees either. You are being evicted from your village because you cannot pay the landlord, which will leave you homeless and vulnerable.

But what if I told you that there was a hidden treasure that belonged to you, and I showed you where it was. Would you remain hungry? Would you let your family die of sickness? Would you let your children continue to be uneducated, homeless, and vulnerable? Or would you use the treasure that was given to you to provide for their needs?

Each person said that they would use the treasure. They knew that this was a spiritual teaching not related to the earthly examples that were used. I explained that this treasure is the Dunamis (resurrection) power of the Most-High God that lives within all who receive Jesus Christ as Savior. As this power is acknowledged, it can be utilized in our lives. We then become a powerful force against the devil, and curses are broken off us- not only witchcraft curses but generational curses as well.

I told them a story about Paul and me being in a situation of not knowing about something that was available to us. Once we found out about it, we never went without it again.

The story is as follows: We were on our first mission's trip in Uganda. It was February of 2016. We were staying in the place we now call home in Uganda. As I have mentioned before, it is the Kitega Community Centre near Lugazi in Kitega Village. Our visits are usually about two months at a time.

The home is westernized as much as it can be to provide a comfortable stay for volunteers. There is electricity in the house, but it often goes out. There is also running water most of the time. We have the luxury of an actual toilet instead of a long drop- a luxury that I am forever grateful for! A long drop is a hole that you squat over to use the bathroom.

The climate is very hot in the dry season, and air conditioning is non-existent. The only thing that is bone chilling cold in Uganda is the water that comes out of the faucets however, it is not potable. The fact that we even have water to stand under while we are there is incredible. The villagers have no such thing as running water. They need to walk miles to get water and carry it home in plastic containers.

You would think that it would feel refreshing with the climate being so hot, but it is quite the contrary. The first six nights we took freezing cold showers. Paul never complains about any of the accommodations, but when he said, "The water is so cold that it hurts," I was relieved that it wasn't just me, and I prayed for wisdom. Then, I had a great idea, or should I say a God idea? I asked the overseer at the Kitega Community Centre if I could use the kettle. He said, "Of course you can use the kettle. Would you like some hot tea?"

Well, I am from Southeast Louisiana, and we drink sweetened Iced Tea. Besides, I could not drink anything heated while in such a hot climate. My response was "Oh no, I want to heat the water and use it to take a warm wipe down bath. Then I will pour it over me to rinse off." His reply floored me. He said, "Cheryl, all you have to do is turn the water heater on for ten minutes before you shower." I said, "WE HAVE A WATER HEATER?!" He simply laughed and brought me to the power switch. He turned it on and said, "You can have a warm shower in ten minutes." I think those were the greatest words that I heard that whole week!

I would turn that same power switch on every day as I was trying to put the bathroom light on. When the light didn't come on, I would simply turn the one next to it on.

The entire time we were there, we had hot water available! The power source was at our fingertips. We just had no idea. I will tell you this: we have never taken another freezing cold shower again. We took the knowledge of having a water heater and used the power source, the switch that was already provided for us, and took warm showers from that day on.

And so it is, with the Dunamis, miracle working, resurrection power of God! It has already been given to you, but you did not know it. Now that you have been told about it and shown through scripture, will you use that power in your own life and apply it to the lives of others? Or will you let it lie dormant?

Although the Dunamis power was not going to miraculously pay their landlord, school fees, or medicine, it was a revelation that they could relate to by using those things as an example. This opened their eyes of understanding to receive the rest of the teachings on how to access and use this great power in the spiritual realm.

We were able to teach pastors, bishops, congregations, and community leaders how to pray effectively. They have seen tremendous changes through the power of God working in their lives.

There will be a testimony at the end of this book that will shed some light on what has been taught here.

CHAPTER SIXTEEN
KNOWLEDGE & AUTHORITY IN CHRIST

The power of God and authority in Christ is for all Christians. It is not denominationally determined. It is not a "holy roller" thing as many people perceive. The only stipulation is to be born again, which is a sincere, heartfelt prayer. This prayer does not change your "religion." To be born again you can pray:

> *"Heavenly Father, I am a sinner, and I ask you to forgive me of my sins. I believe that Jesus Christ is Your only begotten Son, miraculously conceived and born of the virgin Mary. I acknowledge that He was crucified, died, and was buried, and on the third day He rose again. I acknowledge that He did this for me. I receive Jesus as my personal Lord and Savior this very moment. Holy Spirit, come and live within me, guide me, and fill me with power from on high. In Jesus' Name, I pray, Amen."*
>
> **John 14:6 (NIV) "Jesus answered, 'I am the way and the truth and the life. No one comes to the Father except through me.'"**

Simply reading and reciting something that is written has no power. But if you prayed that prayer and meant it, you have become born again. Perhaps you felt something when you prayed, and maybe you did not feel anything. We cannot go by feelings. If you prayed, and accepted Jesus as your Savior, then you are born again, and all that has been discussed here belongs to you. There will be a change in your life and your perspective as you embrace the scriptures.

Spending time with Jesus, reading His Word, and seeking His will for your life will cause your faith to grow. You must then put your faith into action so that you can have victory over the devil and lead others to victory as well.

Is a newborn baby able to walk, talk and care for himself? Can a person who has never driven before just get behind the wheel of a car and drive it safely? Can a person who has never attended medical school perform a successful surgery?

Those answers are all an emphatic no! They must first be taught then trained. They can only perfect what they have learned through much practice.

We have become people who want the benefits, but we do not want to put in the work. I encourage you today to study the scriptures, inquire of the Lord, and let Him lead and direct you. He is not some distant God who is too busy for you. In the same manner that you talk to your best friend, talk to Him. No need to rehearse or recite what to say. Just speak to Him from your heart. He is eagerly listening.

To walk in the Power that The Lord has freely given us, we must know His Word so we can learn how to fight in the spiritual realm. I was personally tired of always feeling defeated. Nothing ever seemed to go right for me- that is, until I learned God's Word and how to apply it to my life.

2 Timothy 2:15 "Study to show thyself approved unto God, a workman that needeth not to be ashamed, rightly dividing the word of truth."

2 Corinthians 10: 3-5 (NIV) "For though we live in the world, we do not wage war as the world does. The weapons we fight with are not the weapons of the world. On the contrary, they have *divine power to demolish strongholds*. We demolish arguments and every pretension that sets itself up against the knowledge of God, and we take captive every thought to make it obedient to Christ." (Italics added)

Notice how many times this scripture says "we." The Lord has equipped us through His Word to be successful. *We* just need to do our part.

Ephesians 6:10-11(NIV) "Finally, be strong in the Lord and *in his mighty power*. Put on the full armor of God, so that you can take your stand against the devil's schemes." (Italics added)

AUTHORITY IN CHRIST JESUS

As believers in Christ, it is important that we know the authority we have in Him. We have seen so far that we are called to be Overcomers. We have learned about the Power of the Blood of Jesus, and also discovered that the Dunamis, miracle-working, resurrection Power of God has been placed inside of us.

But now, it is time to exercise the Authority that God has given to us. When we put all these incredible pieces together, we will be operating in the fullness that He intended, and we will see miracles in our lives. Generational curses will be broken, and the wounds in our souls will begin to heal.

All scripture is God breathed, so when we read scripture, it is a fact and not a suggestion. The following scriptures talk about the authority we have in Christ:

Matthew 28:18-20 (NKJV) "And Jesus came and spoke to them, saying, "*All authority* has been given to Me in heaven and on earth. *Go* therefore and make disciples of all the nations, baptizing them in the name of the Father and of the Son and of the Holy Spirit, teaching them to observe all things that I have commanded you; and lo, I am with you always, *even* to the end of the age. Amen." (Italics added)

Luke 9:1-2 (NIV) "When Jesus had called the Twelve together, he gave them *power and authority* to drive out *all* demons and to cure diseases, and he sent them out to proclaim the kingdom of God and to heal those who were ill." (Italics added)

Mark 16:17-18 (NIV) "And these signs will accompany those who believe: In my name they will drive out demons; they will speak in new tongues; they will pick up snakes with their hands; and when they drink deadly poison, it will not hurt them at all; they will place their hands on sick people, and they will get well."

Luke 10:19 (NIV) "I have given you authority to trample on snakes and scorpions and to overcome *all* the power of the enemy; nothing will harm you." (Italics added)

1 Corinthains 15:57 (NIV) "But thanks be to God! He gives us the victory through our Lord Jesus Christ."

Ephesians 6:10-11 (NIV) "Finally, be strong in the Lord and in *his mighty power*. Put on the full armor

of God, so that you can take your stand against the devil's schemes." (Italics added)

2 Thessalonians 3:3 (NKJV) "But the Lord is faithful, who will establish you and guard you from the evil one."

Fear is what holds many people back from fully operating in the power and authority of God. A tactic of the devil is to instill fear in our lives so that we will not step out in faith. This fear will stop the blessings of God from ever reaching us. I encourage you to be strong and be bold, and you will be victorious!

2 Timothy 1:6-7 (NKJV) "Therefore I remind you to stir up the gift of God which is in you through the laying on of my hands. For God has not given us a spirit of fear, but of power and of love and of a sound mind."

John 10:10 (NKJV) "The thief does not come except to steal, and to kill and to destroy. I have come that they may have life and that they may have it more abundantly."

Notice that this scripture says, "have it more abundantly." This means nothing missing and nothing broken in our lives.

The first thing the devil comes to steal is our joy. Joy is a fruit of the Holy Spirit. It does not make sense in the natural mind. When we become born again, there is a deep joy in our souls knowing that we are destined for heaven. Joy and happiness are not the same. Joy can remain in the hardest of times because it is not circumstantial like happiness. It is spiritual.

Have you noticed that when bad things happen, we immediately feel the dread of the circumstances? Dread comes in like a flood and completely overtakes our thinking. Our *happiness* is taken immediately, but we must hold on to the Joy of the Lord that comes with our assurance of salvation. The reason the thief, the devil, goes after our joy is because he wants us to forget who we are in Christ, and he knows that the joy of the Lord is our strength. Let the following scriptures be the cry of your heart when all joy seems to have faded:

> **Nehemiah 8:10 (NKJV) "Do not sorrow, the joy of the Lord is your strength."**

> **Psalm 51:12 "Restore unto me the joy of Thy salvation; and uphold me with Thy free spirit."**

The second thing the devil attempts to do is to kill your faith because he knows that without faith it is impossible to please God. Since the Holy Spirit dwells within you, your faith is not easily destroyed, so do not panic. It may feel like it is gone, but Jesus is always at the right hand of the Father making intercession for you, and the family of believers are praying for you as well.

> **Hebrews 11:1 (NKJV) "Now faith is the substance of things hoped for, the evidence of things not seen."**

> **Hebrews 11:6. "But without faith it is impossible to please him: for he that cometh to God must believe that he is, and that he is a rewarder of them that diligently seek him."**

Jesus told us in His Word about the power of mustard seed faith in the book of Matthew. Having moments or even seasons of doubt or unbelief does not mean we have lost our faith, although it may feel that way.

> **Matthew 17:20-21** "And Jesus said unto them, Because of your unbelief: for verily I say unto you, if ye have faith as a grain of mustard seed, ye shall say unto this mountain, Remove hence to yonder place; and it shall remove; and nothing shall be impossible unto you."

Notice in the scripture above that Jesus said, "Because of your unbelief: for verily I say unto you…" He knew they were struggling and had to let them know that with faith as small as the grain of mustard seed, they could accomplish much. He brought a new perspective to them.

The mustard seed is one of the smallest seeds, and it grows into an immense tree, often as tall as thirty feet! In your times of trouble, you may lose the desire or even strength to pray, but your mustard seed faith is still there.

> **Matthew 13:31-32** "Another parable put he forth unto them, saying, The kingdom of heaven is like to a grain of mustard seed, which a man took, and sowed in his field: Which indeed is the least of all seeds: but when it is grown, it is greatest among herbs, and becometh a tree, so that the birds of the air come and lodge in the branches therof."

You can confidently stand firm knowing that mustard seed faith is within you, and just as a mustard tree cannot just be pushed over, neither can your faith.

Lastly, the devil schemes to destroy your hope. There are so many scriptures on hope, but I will only list a few. I challenge you to do a study on this subject. You will find a *renewed hope* through His Word.

Jeremiah 29:11(NIV) "'For I know the plans I have for you,' declares the Lord, 'plans to prosper you and not to harm you, plans to give you hope and a future.'"

Romans 15:13 (NKJV) "Now may the God of hope fill you with all joy and peace in believing, that you may abound in hope by the power of the Holy Spirit."

Proverbs 23:18 (NIV) "There is surely a future hope for you, and your hope will not be cut off."

It is time that we take our rightful place as sons and daughters of the Most- High God and stand on His Word against all the attacks of the devil.

Isaiah 59:19 (NIV) "When the enemy comes in like a flood, the Spirit of the Lord shall raise up a standard against him."

Peter 5:6-9 (NIV) "Be alert and of sober mind. Your enemy the devil prowls around *like* a roaring lion looking for someone to devour. Resist him, standing firm in the faith, because you know that the family of believers throughout the world is undergoing the same kind of sufferings."

This scripture says, "Your enemy the devil prowls around **like** a roaring lion." Oh! But we know the Lion of the Tribe of Judah, and that Lion is on our side- Hallelujah!

It's time we say ENOUGH DEVIL! I choose to walk in the Victory of my Lord and Savior Jesus Christ!

My prayer for you is that you have been equipped through the Word of God to press on toward complete healing in your life- body, soul, and spirit. You are now fully informed of the Power of the Blood, the Dunamis Power that lives inside of you, and the Authority you have in Christ.

Numbers 6:24-26 "The Lord bless thee and keep thee: The Lord make his face shine upon thee, and be gracious to thee: The Lord lift up his countenance upon thee and give thee peace."

CHAPTER SEVENTEEN
APPLICATION AND ACTIVATION

When you get that phone call, the knock on the door that changes everything, or the doctor's report that sends fear surging through your veins, it's easy to spin out of control into a full-blown panic.

My prayer is that you can take the information I've given you and reverse the panic into praise. There is nothing too difficult for the Lord.

It is truly amazing how the pastors and bishops open their pulpits for us to preach and teach in their countries. They are not only eager to learn for themselves, but also for their congregations to learn how to be effective in prayer through the shed blood of Christ, the Dunamis/Resurrection power of God, and the Authority we have in Him.

Miracles happen in Africa because these precious people hear the Word of God and believe it instantly. They do not second guess the scriptures. Evil has encamped them for generations, and when given the knowledge on how to overcome evil through the Word of God, they take the authority and receive their victory.

All too often, we go to God in prayer with repetition when what He desires to hear is the sincere, wholehearted prayers of His people. We need not beg Him to answer prayers. Let's turn those prayers into the effectual, fervent prayers that God desires.

Fervent- "very hot: glowing: exhibiting or marked by great intensity of feeling: zealous." (Merriam-Webster)

Next, we will not only learn how to pray fervently but also with power. The key to having powerful prayers is by applying all the elements together.

The blood of Jesus, the Dunamis power of God, and the Authority that we have been given, are essential in seeing sickness and disease annihilated, generational curses and addictions broken forever, relationships restored, and financial breakthroughs happen. Whatever the circumstance, prayer is the answer. First, we must learn the proper way to pray.

> **John 15:6 "You did not choose Me but I chose you, and appointed you that you should go and bear fruit and that your fruit should abide, so that *whatever you ask of the Father in My name* He may give to you."** (Italics added)

> **John 16:23-24 (NAS) "In that day you will not question Me about anything. Truly, truly, I say to you, *if you ask the Father for anything in My name*, He will give it to you. Until now you have asked for nothing in My name; ask and you will receive, so that your joy may be made full."** (Italics added)

We are to pray to the Father in Jesus' name. This is a basic guideline for prayer. Let the Lord lead you as you begin this journey into a whole new prayer life.

Example Prayers:

> *Heavenly Father, I come to you in Jesus' name. I ask you to cover me in the precious blood of Jesus that was shed for me on the cross. I lay (my sickness, disease, broken relationship, children, finances, job, etc. name the situation) at your feet. I plead the blood of Jesus over (name*

the situation) right now. I know that I have the same Dunamis/Resurrection power that rose Jesus from the grave living inside of me, and I send that power to the source of this situation. Holy Spirit, I ask you to intervene and turn this situation around for Your glory. I use my God given authority, and I command all demonic attacks against me in this situation (name it) to CEASE AND DESIST RIGHT NOW! I thank you, Father, for hearing and answering me. In Jesus Name, AMEN.

If you or someone you are praying for is struggling with a certain sickness, name the sickness and command it to cease and desist.

If it is cancer, call it by name and command it to die at the roots in Jesus' name. The same is true with any other ailment.

If you are struggling financially, command the spirit of poverty to be broken in the name of Jesus. Then thank the Lord for bringing in financial wisdom and provision from all directions.

For your children, loved ones, and friends, command the enemy to loose them in Jesus' Name. Then thank the Lord for touching their lives.

There is no situation too hard for the blood of Jesus, the Dunamis/Resurrection power of God, and the Authority in Christ to change.

For generational curses of sickness, behaviors, addictions, etc. you will want to write a list. In this list, include everything that you can think of that has affected people in your bloodline.

In my bloodline, I had an array of generational curses of sickness and diseases on the list- the very things that the doctor asks for in the "Family History" like heart disease, cancer, high blood pressure, diabetes, high cholesterol, high triglycerides, migraines, and fatty liver.

In my family, there was premature high blood pressure starting as young as fifteen years old in several family members as well as the entire list above.

> *Heavenly Father, in the name of Jesus, I plead the blood of Jesus over all heart disease in my lineage. I send forth the Dunamis power of God to all heart disease. I command with the authority of the Most-High God that the curse of heart disease be broken all the way back to Adam. Broken from my lineage, broken off me, my children, and all future generations in Jesus' Name. Amen!*

Please notice that I said, "All the way back to Adam." This goes all the way back to the beginning of mankind. We were all created through the lineage of Adam. We do not want to leave any open doors.

Concerning addictions:

> *Heavenly Father, in the name of Jesus, I plead the blood of Jesus over all alcoholism in my lineage. I send forth the Dunamis power of God to all alcoholism. I command with the authority of the Most-High God, that the curse of alcoholism be broken all the way back to Adam! Broken from my lineage, broken off me, my children, and all future generations in Jesus' Name. Amen!*

In most families that deal with addictions, you can see the pattern throughout the lineage. This does not mean everyone has that addiction. It means that the curse is there, lying dormant, and it leaves an open door to pounce on any certain individual in that bloodline. For some families, it skips a generation but will manifest in another.

Some people deal with "ghost like" things happening around their home. This is nothing more than familiar spirits. It is demonic and must be dealt with. Oftentimes, someone with experience needs to be called in to get these entities out of their home or off their property. The familiar spirits can be from people who lived there many years ago and have nothing to do with your family.

When my son was a toddler, he had an "Imaginary Friend" named Michael. He would play with the toys in his room for hours with Michael. At lunch time he would have me set out a plate for him with imaginary food on it. Having no spiritual knowledge at the time, I thought it was cute. My sister Patti had a boyfriend named Michael, and he loved spending time with my son. I figured he named his imaginary friend after her boyfriend.

This went on for over a year. One day, while at my in-law's house, my father-in-law asked me to clean out the closet in the spare room. As I was pulling boxes out, there was a picture of a young boy. My son grabbed the picture and said, "MOM! This is Michael." My mother-in-law ran into the room, and her face was pale. She said, "Let me see that." I asked her, "Who is the young boy in the picture?" She said, "That is my son, Michael! He died at six years old."

That imaginary friend never appeared to my son again. This was a familiar spirit, and it had been identified. By the grace of God that familiar spirit left, which is not always the case without spiritual intervention.

Concerning your home or property, (if you are confident in doing this, otherwise seek help) whether you own the property or not:

Heavenly Father, in the name of Jesus, I thank You for the power and authority that You have given to me to cast out devils. I plead the blood of Jesus over my home/ property. With the Dunamis Power of the Most-High God I command every familiar spirit in or around this property to leave in the Mighty Name of Jesus. You are not welcome here. This home is dedicated to the Lord Jesus Christ, and you must flee!

These are sample prayers. You will put in whatever sickness, disease, addiction, behavior, etc. that is affecting you or your family members. You can look back at the list previously written. Keep in mind that grudges, offenses, unforgiveness, bitterness, anger, and revenge are passed down in the lineage as well.

CHAPTER EIGHTEEN

SCRIPTURES TO DECLARE OVER YOUR LIFE

Personalize these declarations with scripture references for yourself and your loved ones. Parentheses added when personalized.

Colossians 1:13-14 (NIV) "For he has rescued us (me) from the dominion of darkness and brought us (me) into the kingdom of the Son he loves, in whom we (I) have redemption, the forgiveness of sins."

Romans 8:37-39 (NIV) "No, in all these things we (I am) are more than conquerors through him who loved us (me). For I am convinced that neither death nor life, neither angels nor demons, neither the present nor the future, nor any powers, neither height nor depth, nor anything else in all creation, will be able to separate us (me) from the love of God that is in Christ Jesus our (my) Lord."

Ephesians 6:10—I am strong in the Lord and in the power of His might

Acts 26:18 – My eyes are open. I turn from darkness to light, and I am delivered from the power of Satan into the hands of God.

Luke 5:17- Impart Your power in healing and deliverance through me.

Luke 9:43- Lord, I am amazed at Your great power.

Acts 4:33- Let Your great power and grace be released through me like it was through Your apostles.

Romans 15:19–Let signs, wonders and miracles through the power of the Holy Spirit be released upon me.

1 Corinthians 2:4- Let me preach and teach with a demonstration of the Spirit's power.

Ephesians 3:20- Let Your power work within me.

Luke 1:17- May I go forth in the spirit and power of Elijah.

Scripture references and declarations on the Power of the Blood

Revelation 12:11- I have the victory over the devil through the blood of Jesus.

1 Peter 1:2–I am covered in the blood of Jesus, and I receive an abundance of grace and peace.

Hebrews 13: 20-21- I am fully equipped to do God's will through the blood of Jesus Christ.

Hebrews 10:17- I am forgiven through the blood of Jesus.

Hebrews 10:19- I can boldly enter God's presence through the blood of Jesus.

Hebrews 9:14- My conscience is cleansed from dead works through the blood of Jesus.

Ephesians 1:7- I have been redeemed through the blood of Jesus.

Matthew 26:28- I receive the forgiveness of the new covenant through the blood of Jesus.

1 John 1:7- The blood of Jesus cleanses me from all sin.

Colossians 1:20- I have been reconciled unto Christ, and I have peace through the blood of Jesus.

CHAPTER NINETEEN
TESTIMONY OF THE POWER OF PRAYER

During our 2020 visit in Uganda, we heard about a girl who was sixteen years old. She was the youth worship leader in her church. The Sunday that I preached there, I was amazed at how beautifully she sang. My teachings in Africa were always messages of encouragement, but they were about to shift after what happened shortly thereafter.

Two weeks after I preached in her church, we received word that a witch put a curse on her. Witches and witch doctors are all throughout the villages. There are many language barriers, but I will explain what was told to me, and I pray that it is accurately portrayed here.

The teacher called her to the front of the class. Her classmates were told to line up and thank her one by one for getting the highest grade in the class. The teacher then told the other students that since she got a better test score than all of them, they were thanking her for a beating that they would be getting. The teacher proceeded to beat her classmates.

One of the students was a witch. She put a curse on this sweet girl, and severe headaches began immediately. The headaches only came when she walked into the school. As soon as she walked out, the headaches stopped. She continued to go to school every day even though she was suffering. This did not make the witch happy. The intention was to keep her from coming to school altogether. The witch decided to increase the curse. Along with the headaches, she put a curse of blindness on her.

The next morning, she woke up blind. She was now bound to her own home, exactly what the witch wanted in the first place. Once we were told about what happened, Paul began interceding, and I went to her home on the other side of the village.

Our interpreter, a faithful woman of God, guided me on the very long walk in the late evening. I knew I had to see her at once. I was able to share with her, her mother, and sister the teachings that I have taught in this book about the Blood, the Power, and the Authority that we have in Jesus Christ as weapons against the devil.

I asked her if she believed, and if she understood what I just taught her. She said yes, so I said, "Then let's break that curse!" The Holy Spirit filled the room, and everyone knew it. She felt her eyes change when I was praying and commanding the curse to be broken in the Name of Jesus. She participated in the prayer as well, commanding as I taught her. Although the presence of God was very strong, she was afraid to remove the blindfold.

In the short time that she was blind from the curse, she found refuge behind the blindfold. The glare hurt her eyes when they were not covered. I told her, "The curse has been broken. Now you must trust the Lord." She was still gripped with fear, so we prayed over that, too. I did not force her to remove the blindfold that evening. I asked her to promise me that in the morning, she would at least peek through.

Being that she lived quite a distance away, I knew there was a chance that I would never see her again. I also knew that the Lord did His part in healing her, and now it was her turn to exercise her faith.

About three weeks later, a missionary from Scotland, who was staying at the Kitega Community Centre with us, went to the girl's church for a Sunday morning service. When she returned to the Center after the service, she said, "The young girl was giving her testimony today about being healed from the curse of blindness!" Praise God!

We were in Africa for two months, and every weekend, we ministered in a different Village church. If the missionary from Scotland had not been in that certain church service, we would not have had confirmation of her healing before we came back to America.

Paul and I visited her family in 2023 and found out that she is in a university pursuing a promising career. What is truly amazing is that she never lost her joy. Even with blind eyes, she had the joy of the Lord through the entire ordeal. Was she outwardly happy? No, but she never lost the joy of His salvation in her life.

I am so grateful that she exercised her faith and removed that blindfold. The devil would have loved nothing more than to have her convinced, through fear, that she was blind for the rest of her life when she could see all along. Too many Christians are crippled by the lies of the enemy, crippling them from their destiny. It is time to change that!

After the experience with this sweet girl, I shifted into teaching God's people in Africa how to war against the darkness through the Blood of Jesus, the Dunamis Power of God, and the Authority we have in Christ.

CHAPTER TWENTY

JUST AS ELIJAH - DESIRING DEATH IN DESPAIR

In a previous chapter, I shared the story of Elijah. He was so stricken by fear and despair that he genuinely desired death as a way of escape from the serious attacks against him. Please understand that God never intended that man should take his own life, regardless of the circumstances he finds himself in. There is always help for those struggling with such desires. It is important to reach out to family, friends, pastors, and professionals trained in this area.

What I am about to share may strike up controversy, but we must apply the Word of God to the situation and not rely on our old ways of thinking. This is just my perspective on a very delicate subject. Only God knows the outcome of each person. No one should ever gamble with eternity by doing such a thing as taking their own life.

While we were in Uganda, a well-known man of God committed suicide. This man diligently served the Lord, and he raised his children in Christ. One of his children is a Lay Minister in the surrounding villages. He was a forerunner to church planting. He would find and secure land for churches to be built on. He was a well-respected man throughout their region who loved the Lord with all his heart.

As his wife was preparing dinner, he went out to the back of his house. When the food was served, his wife went to look for him, and she found him hanging from a tree. He had taken the rope from their goat and used it for his death.

There was no indication that he was in a suicidal condition. It could be looked upon as a sign of weakness to reach out for help, so he suffered in silence until he reached utter despair.

As is the law in Uganda, the body of a suicide victim cannot be touched until the police arrive. Family and villagers gather around in mourning as the person hangs from the tree.

Very sadly, the custom is for a hole to be dug underneath the body, and the police brutally beat the body as it is hanging. Everyone in attendance watches this terrible beating take place. Next, the rope is cut, the body drops down into the hole and is covered up. However the body falls into the hole is the way it is buried.

The family is not allowed to take their loved one down, dress him, or place him in a casket. In their custom, a person who takes his own life is not worthy of a proper burial.

This is extremely traumatic for the family and for those who are watching. The intent is to scare everyone in attendance from ever committing suicide.

Thankfully, because of the respect that this man had in his community, the police allowed the family to remove him from the rope and place him into a casket after the beating. He was buried in the same place that he took his own life.

When my husband Paul and I heard about this, we knew that we had to go minister to this family. It took about a week before our interpreter was able to get in touch with a family member and set up a meeting. Their grief was crushing to them. Suicide is not very common in Uganda, and for it to be a man of God was even more unbelievable to these God-fearing people.

We had been teaching about the Body, Soul, and Spirit for over a month at this point. We knew that we had to get these teachings to them. Here was a man who loved Jesus. He served the Lord and was instrumental in building the kingdom of God. The devil brought discouragement and despair upon him just as Elijah had experienced. He infiltrated the man's thoughts and brought him to a desperate place.

The devil could not stop him from serving the Lord, and he could not take his spirit to hell. The only tactic the devil had was to torment him in his mind. Out of desperation, his act of self-will caused him to take his own life as a way of escaping from the torment.

Remember, the soul of man is the mind, will, and emotions. This attack of the devil ended this man's Kingdom work here on earth. His physical body was destroyed through the torment of his mind, but his spirit belonged to the Lord. He served the Lord, the communities, and built Christian Churches. He was always an encourager.

The only way to lose our salvation is to reject Christ and turn away from Him. This man never renounced Jesus or walked away from his calling. He served the Lord until his last breath here on earth. The devil comes to steal, kill, and destroy. He penetrated this servant's thoughts and drove him to do the unthinkable. I cannot imagine the torment he was going through.

The Lord does not leave those who are struggling.

Romans 8:38-39 "For I am convinced that neither death nor life, neither angels nor demons, neither the present nor the future, nor any powers, neither height nor depth, nor anything else in all creation, will be able to separate us from the love of God that is in Christ Jesus our Lord."

Romans 10:10-13 "For it is with your heart that you believe and are justified, and it is with your mouth that you profess your faith and are saved. As Scripture says, 'Anyone who believes in him will never be put to shame' For there is no difference between Jew and Gentile—the same Lord is Lord of all and richly

blesses all who call on him, for, 'Everyone who calls on the name of the Lord will be saved.'"

Am I implying "once saved always saved?" Absolutely not. We cannot simply say the sinner's prayer and live a life of sin thinking that we are heaven bound no matter what we do in life. What I am implying is that just because a believer is viciously attacked by the devil and does the unthinkable act of suicide to escape the agony does not necessarily mean they are in hell. Only the Lord knows the intentions and heart of all mankind, but once again, we should never gamble with eternity. Always reach out for help!

Our continued prayer for the family and the community that deeply loved him is that they can find peace in the scriptures and allow their souls to be restored from this pain.

I also pray that the Lord begins restoring your soul. May you allow Him into the deep recesses of your pain where only He can fully heal you of every situation in your life, the things you know about and the things that you don't. He will go all the way back through the generations and free you and your children and all future generations from the curses that lie dormant.

There is never a reason to despair to the point of wanting to die. The Lord is always with you. His word says in Hebrews 13:5 that He will never leave you nor forsake you.

No matter how deep your pain, call out to Jesus. He is ever present in your time of need. There is no situation that is too ugly, too shameful, or too deep to invite Him into.

Psalm 46:1(NLT) "God is our refuge and strength, always ready to help in times of trouble."

Jesus did not come into the world to condemn the world, as some are in the habit of thinking. God is not a cruel judge waiting to bring down punishment. Instead, He knew that we needed a Savior, and He sent Jesus so that we may have eternal life with Him.

> **Romans 3:23 "For all have sinned and come short of the glory of God."**

> **John 3:16-17 "For God so loved the world, that he gave his only begotten Son, that whosoever believeth in him should not perish, but have everlasting life. For God did not send his Son into the world to condemn the world; but that the world might be saved."**

He came to set us free from sin and condemnation. He loves you, my friends. Embrace the love and grace that He has for you. You are His treasure here on earth. I will leave you with these powerful scriptures, and I pray that you allow Him to restore your soul.

> **3 John 1:2 (AMP) "Beloved, I pray that in every way you may succeed and prosper and be in good health (physically), just as (I know) your soul prospers (spiritually).**

> **1 Corinthians 15:57 "But thanks be to God, which giveth us the victory through our Lord Jesus Christ"**

Perhaps you are interested in a mission's trip away from your hometown but still in America. I have personally had incredible experiences with Christ in Action, a faith-based organization that reaches across the entire United States for disaster relief. I was a recipient of their amazing relief work after Hurricane Katrina destroyed my home. Volunteers make their relief efforts possible. It is so fulfilling being the hands, feet, and mouthpiece of Christ in such dire circumstances. Paul has also volunteered with other organizations like Operation Blessing and Samaritans Purse whom you can contact as well.

Christ In Action – christinaction.com

You may also contact me through one of the following:
Samuelworldwideministries.org

Email:
Pjc34578@gmail.com or Samuelworldwideministries@gmail.com

www.ingramcontent.com/pod-product-compliance
Ingram Content Group UK Ltd.
Pitfield, Milton Keynes, MK11 3LW, UK
UKHW032333131224
452011UK00004B/53